PRAISE FOR THE
UNCOMMON JUNIO.

The *Uncommon* Junior High curriculum will help God's Word to become real for your students.

Larry Acosta
Founder of the Hispanic Ministry Center, Urban Youth Workers Institute

The best junior high/middle school curriculum to come out in years.

Jim Burns, Ph.D.
President of HomeWord (www.homeword.com)

A rich resource that makes genuine connections with middle school students and the culture in which they live.

Mark W. Cannister
Professor of Christian Ministries, Gordon College, Wenham, Massachusetts

A landmark resource for years to come.

Chapman R. Clark, Ph.D.
Professor of Youth, Family and Culture, Fuller Theological Seminary

Great biblical material, creative interaction and *user friendly*! What more could you ask for? I highly recommend it!

Ken Davis
Author and Speaker (www.kendavis.com)

A fresh tool . . . geared to make a lasting impact.

Paul Fleischmann
President and Co-founder of the National Network of Youth Ministries

The *Uncommon* Junior High curriculum capitalizes both GOD and TRUTH.

Monty L. Hipp
President, The C4 Group (www.c4group.nonprofitsites.com)

The *Uncommon* Junior High curriculum is truly cross-cultural.

Walt Mueller
Founder and President, Center for Parent/Youth Understanding (www.cpyu.org)

The creators and writers of this curriculum know and love young teens, and that's what sets good junior high curriculum apart from the mediocre stuff!

Mark Oestreicher
Author, Speaker and Consultant (www.markoestreicher.com)

This is serious curriculum for junior-highers! Not only does it take the great themes of the Christian faith seriously, but it takes junior-highers seriously as well.

Wayne Rice
Founder and Director, Understanding Your Teenager (www.waynerice.com)

The *Uncommon* Junior High curriculum fleshes out two absolute essentials for great curriculum: biblical depth and active learning.

Duffy Robbins
Professor of Youth Ministry, Eastern University, St. Davids, Pennsylvania

It's about time that curriculum took junior-highers and youth workers seriously.

Rich Van Pelt
President of Alongside Consulting, Denver, Colorado

The *Uncommon* Junior High curriculum will help leaders bring excellence to every lesson while enjoying the benefit of a simplified preparation time.

Lynn Ziegenfuss
Mentoring Project Director, National Network of Youth Ministries

uncommon

DEALING WITH PRESSURE AND CHANGE

KARA POWELL
General Editor

Published by Gospel Light
Ventura, California, U.S.A.
www.gospellight.com
Printed in the U.S.A.

Unit 1, "Dealing with Pressure," previously published as Pulse #7: Life at School.
Unit 2, "Dealing with Change," never before published.

Contributing writers: Kara Powell, Ph.D., Natalie Chenault, Donna Fitzpatrick,
Paul Fleischmann, Siv Ricketts and Amy Simpson.

Library of Congress Cataloging-in-Publication Data
Uncommon jr. high group study : dealing with pressure and change /
Kara Powell, General Editor.
p. cm.
Includes bibliographical references and index.
ISBN 978-0-8307-6091-6 (trade paper : alk. paper)
1. Church group work with teenagers. 2. Junior high school students—Conduct of life—
Study and teaching. 3. Junior high school students—Religious life—Study and teaching.
4. Stress in adolescence—Religious aspects—Christianity—Study and teaching.
5. Change (Psychology)—Religious aspects—Christianity—Study and teaching.
I. Powell, Kara Eckmann, 1970- II. Title: Uncommon junior high group study.
III. Title: Dealing with pressure and change.
BV4447.U5435 2012
268'.433—dc23
2012013610

Rights for publishing this book outside the U.S.A. or in non-English languages are
administered by Gospel Light Worldwide, an international not-for-profit ministry.
For additional information, please visit www.glww.org, email info@glww.org, or write
to Gospel Light Worldwide, 1957 Eastman Avenue, Ventura, CA 93003, U.S.A.

To order copies of this book and other Gospel Light products in bulk quantities,
please contact us at 1-800-446-7735.

Contents

How to Use the Uncommon Junior High Group Studies

Each *Uncommon* junior high group study contains 12 sessions, which are divided into 2 stand-alone units of 6 sessions each. You may choose to teach all 12 sessions consecutively, or to use just one unit, or to present each session separately. You know your group, so do what works best for you and your students.

This is your leader's guidebook for teaching your group. Electronic files (in PDF format) for each session's student handouts are available online at **www.gospellight.com/uncommon/jh_dealing_with_pressure.zip.** The handouts include the "Reflect" section of each study, formatted for easy printing, in addition to any student worksheets for the session. You may print as many copies as you need for your group.

Each individual session begins with a brief overview of the "big idea" of the lesson, the aims of the session, the primary Bible verse and additional verses that tie in to the topic being discussed. Each of the 12 sessions is geared to be 45 to 90 minutes in length and is comprised of two options that you can choose from, based on the type of group that you have. Option 1 tends to be a more active learning experience, while Option 2 tends to be a more discussion-oriented exercise.

The sections in each session are as follows:

Starter
Young people will stay in your youth group longer if they feel comfortable and make friends. This first section helps students get to know each other better and focus on the theme of the lesson in a fun and engaging way.

Message
The Message section enables students to look up to God by relating the words of Scripture to the session topic.

Dig

Unfortunately, many young people are biblically illiterate. In this section, students look inward and discover how God's Word connects with their own world.

Apply

Young people need the opportunity to think through the issues at hand. The apply section leads students out into their world with specific challenges to apply at school, at home and with their friends.

Reflect

This concluding section of the study allows students to reflect on the material presented in the session. You can print these pages from the PDF found at **www.gospellight.com/uncommon/jh_dealing_with_pressure.zip** and give them to your students as a handout for them to work on throughout the week.

Want More Options?

An additional option for each section, along with accompanying worksheets, is available in PDF format at **www.gospellight.com/uncommon/jh_dealing_with_pressure.zip**.

UNIT I

Dealing with Pressure

It is well with my soul.

Odds are good that when you or your students hear that phrase, you think of the familiar hymn. While I have always loved that hymn, I have come to appreciate it even more as I have learned its history.

In the 1860s, Horatio Spafford and his wife, Anna, were faithful Christians as well as prominent members of society in Chicago. Yet neither their faith nor their wealth spared them from catastrophe. In 1871, their only son was killed by scarlet fever at age four. Shortly after, the many of the properties and buildings they owned were damaged in the Great Chicago Fire.

To give his family some much-needed rest, Horatio and Anna decided to head to England for a holiday, so they booked tickets on an ocean liner for them and their four daughters. Shortly before they were to board the ship, some business developments demanded Horatio's attention, and he felt he needed to stay in the United States. Not wanting to ruin their family's vacation, Anna and the girls decided to head for England. Horatio would follow shortly behind.

On November 2, 1873, the ship ferrying Anna and her four daughters crashed into another ship. Twelve minutes later, the ship sank, dragging the four daughters to their death in the deep ocean sea. When Horatio heard the news, he immediately boarded another ship to meet up with his wife in England. As his ship chugged past the place where his daughters' ship had sank, Horatio wrote these words:

When peace, like a river, attendeth my way,
When sorrows like sea billows roll;
Whatever my lot, Thou hast taught me to say,
It is well, it is well with my soul.

It is well (it is well),
With my soul (with my soul),
It is well, it is well with my soul.

Odds are good that you and the students in your ministry have not experienced the Job-like trauma that Horatio Spafford did. But you've had your own share of challenges and your own unique pressures.

In the midst of the pressures that middle-school students face, it's easy for them to fall into two polar extremes. The first extreme is *denial,* in which they pretend that they don't have any problems. You might ask a student who you know is going through family drama or has an out-of-control schedule how they're doing, and their response will be, "I'm fine," or "I'm doing great".

At the opposite end of the spectrum is *despair.* In the midst of what middle-schoolers are facing, it's easy for them to feel overwhelmed and absent of hope. Students in your ministry can easily be thrown when they don't get invited to a classmate's birthday party or they don't get the grade they hoped for in English.

That's where Horatio's lyrics come in handy. Note that he avoids *denial* by admitting that his sorrows are as large as giant waves in the ocean (a haunting reference to his four daughters' deaths). But he also avoids *despair.* Even in the midst of one of the worst tragedies imaginable, there is a sense of peace and wholeness in Horatio's soul.

May this curriculum offer our students—and us—a sense that whatever we face, it is indeed well with our souls.

Kara Powell
Executive Director of the Fuller Youth Institute
Assistant Professor of Youth, Family and Culture
Fuller Theological Seminary

THE PRESSURE OF SCHOOL

THE BIG IDEA

Prayer can help us deal with any type of stress at school.

SESSION AIMS

In this session, you will guide group members to (1) learn the definition and causes of stress; (2) identify stressful areas in their own lives; and (3) create a plan to deal with the stress in their own lives.

THE BIGGEST VERSES

"Do not be anxious about anything, but in everything, by prayer and petition, with thanksgiving, present your requests to God. And the peace of God, which transcends all understanding, will guard your hearts and your minds in Christ Jesus" (Philippians 4:6-7).

OTHER IMPORTANT VERSES

Genesis 22:1-14; Exodus 1:22–2:4; Ruth 1; 1 Samuel 1:1-17; 2 Kings 22:1–23:3; Job 1:1-22; Psalm 37:7-8; Proverbs 3:5-6; Jeremiah 29:11; Daniel 3:1-30; Matthew 6:25; Luke 12:22-31; John 6:1-15; 1 Thessalonians 5:18

Note: Additional options and worksheets in 8^1/$_2$" x 11" format for this session are available for download at **www.gospellight.com/uncommon/jh_dealing_with_pressure.zip**.

STARTER

Option 1: Stress Level. For this option, you will just need this book! Greet the group members and explain that you will be reading a list of things that might cause a student to have stress at school. Ask the group members to respond to each item by standing and then doing one of the following things:

- If the statement is not stressful to them, they need to put their hands in their pockets (or to their sides) and say, "No stress."
- If the statement causes them a little bit of stress, they need to wave one hand in the air and say, "Some stress."
- If the statement causes them a lot of stress, they need to wave both hands in the air and shout, "Major stress!"

Be sure everyone participates as you read the following list:

- Getting ready for school in the morning
- Going to English class
- Going to gym class
- Going to history class
- Talking to someone you like at lunch
- Forgetting your locker combination
- Getting a pop quiz
- Doing word problems in math
- Spilling your drink on your lap at lunch
- Getting all your homework done
- Going to science class
- Being called to the principal's office
- Being paired with a really popular kid for your science project
- Tripping in the hallway and dropping all your books
- Taking an essay exam
- Finding out you have to write a five-page book report
- Eating mystery meat in the cafeteria
- Tripping at lunch and dropping all your food
- Finding out you've had a booger hanging from your nose for the past half an hour
- Giving an oral report

Invite the students to suggest other possible stress triggers. Transition to the next step by explaining that we all go through stress, but having a relationship with Jesus can help us react differently to it. Our stress level will be lower as we turn stressful situations over to God in prayer.

Option 2: School Stress Melodrama. For this option, you will need one copy of "School Stress Melodrama" (found on the next page) for each of your actors and six chairs. Ahead of time, place the chairs in a traditional classroom setup, angled sideways at the front of the room so the audience can see the group members who will be sitting in them.

Greet the students and let them know that the group will be starting a new series on the pressures that junior-highers face. Choose seven to nine volunteers to perform an impromptu drama. They will need to act out the following roles as you read from the handout:

- Jim, a normal kid dealing with a very stressful day
- Jim's mind, hovering around Jim and making suggestions
- Jim's friends (two to four other group members)
- Jenny, a really popular girl
- Mrs. Cranfield, Jim's math teacher
- Mr. Pritchit, the assistant school principal

Instruct the actors to say the lines on the sheet as you read the melodrama and to act out their parts with enthusiasm.

After the short skit, ask the group members to list the things that they think cause junior-highers stress. (Some answers might include tests, grades, peer acceptance, parental expectations, and so forth.) Explain that today they will be learning how to deal with and overcome the things that stress them out.

MESSAGE

Option 1: Stress Solution. For this option, you will need several Bibles. Begin by dividing the group members into teams of 5 to 10 people. Distribute Bibles and have everyone follow along as you read Job 1:1-3,13-22.[1]

After you have finished reading, instruct each team to put together a 30-second skit in which they will act out the story of Job and offer a solution for the stress he faced. Let the teams know that they must incorporate the primary solution for stress found in verse 21: praying and having the attitude that God is in control. Circulate around the room, making sure the teams understand what they are supposed to be doing and helping them stay on track.

School Stress Melodrama

Characters

Jim, *a normal kid dealing with a stressful day*
Jim's mind, *hovering around Jim and making suggestions*
Jim's friends *(2 to 4 other group members)*

Jenny, *a really popular girl*
Mrs. Cranfield, *Jim's math teacher*
Mr. Pritchit, *the assistant school principal*

It's another day at Pesky Middle School. Jim and his friends are teasing each other and joking around as they make their way to their third period math class. Just before sitting down, Jim trips on his own feet and falls flat on the floor. All of his friends point at him and laugh like crazy.

Mrs. Cranfield, the math teacher, gets mad and snaps at Jim. **"Jim, stop that goofing around and sit down *right this minute!*"**

Jim stands up, straightens out his clothes, and sits down as quickly as he can. Unfortunately, he sits down a bit too quickly, and his chair falls over. Mrs. Cranfield is pretty irritated by now and is convinced that Jim is goofing around. **"Jim, if you don't stop this nonsense, I'm going to call Mr. Pritchit."**

Jim's mind tries to settle him down. *I've got to pull it together. I'm going to pick up my chair, sit down, stop being such a klutz and try to keep a low profile from here on out.*

Jim sits down. But just as he begins to relax, Jenny, a really popular girl at school, walks up to him and says, **"Um, I think you're in my seat."**

Jim is totally embarrassed and jumps up to get out of Jenny's seat. In his hurry, he bumps right into Jenny and knocks all the books out of her arms. Jenny begins to yell at him. All of Jim's friends start laughing again.

By now Mrs. Cranfield is stomping her foot on the floor. **"That's enough, that's enough, that's *enough!*"**

Jim locates another seat, Jenny finally stops yelling, Jim's friends stop laughing, and everything finally seems to be settling down. Then Mrs. Cranfield announces, **"I've got a surprise for you today: a pop quiz!"**

Everyone groans. Jim's mind says, *Why didn't I study last night instead of watching that monster marathon on TV?* He groans even louder than the rest of the class.

Mrs. Cranfield passes out the quiz and tells everyone, **"I insist on complete silence during this test. And absolutely no sharing answers!"**

Jim suddenly realizes that he has to use the restroom—right now! He raises his hand. Mrs. Cranfield impatiently asks, **"What *now*, Jim?"**

Jim says, **"May I be excused to go to the restroom?"** Jim's friends snicker.

Mrs. Cranfield replies, **"Absolutely not! You sit right where you are and finish that quiz. You may leave when you have completed the test."**

Jenny shakes her head and gives Jim a "what planet are you from?" look. Jim nervously squirms in his seat to keep from bursting until he finishes the quiz.

Suddenly, one of Jim's friends whispers to him from across the aisle. **"Hey, Jimbo, what's the answer to number 6?"**

Jim doesn't hear him. He can't seem to focus. His mind is chanting, *Restroom, restroom, gotta go, gotta go.*

Jim's friend says again, a bit louder, **"Jimbo! Hey, Jimbo!"**

Jim's mind is repeating over and over, *Gotta go! Gotta go!*

Jim's friend speaks up again, even a bit louder, **"What's the answer? C'mon, help me out!"**

Jenny is giving Jim that look again.

Jim's mind is screaming, *Restroom! Restroom! Gotta go! Gotta go!*

Jim's friend keeps saying, **"Jimbo, help me out here!"**

Finally, Jim snaps. **"Stop it!" I don't know the answer to number 6!"**

Everyone stops and stares at Jim. Mrs. Cranfield picks up the phone and summons Mr. Pritchit to the classroom.

When Mr. Pritchit arrives, he stands at the front of the room and whispers back and forth with Mrs. Cranfield. Jim's mind says to Jim, *What were you thinking?*

Jim's friends are looking at him like he has lost his mind. Jenny is shaking her hand. Jim tries to disappear by sinking as low as he can into his seat.

Finally, Mr. Pritchit walks over to Jim. He says, **"Let's go, Jim. Looks like you've really done it this time."**

Jim stands up too quickly and bumps into Mr. Pritchit, knocking him into two other students.

Jim's mind says, *Boy, oh boy, you should have stayed in bed this morning!*

Give the teams 10 minutes to prepare their presentations. When they are ready, have them present their skits one at a time. Make sure you (and the rest of the students) give them lots of support and applause for their efforts. Once the skits have been presented, discuss the following questions:

- What do we learn about Job in this story? (*He was a great man who feared God. He was also obedient to God.*)
- What difficult situations caused stress for Job? (*He lost everything—his possessions, his workers and all his children.*)
- Why would losing all of this cause stress? (*Times of pain and loss are extremely stressful!*)
- What was the first thing Job did when he heard this distressing news? (*His first reaction was to worship God.*)
- Did Job try to change the situation right away? (*No.*)
- Did Job grumble or complain? (*No.*)
- Did Job get angry? (*No, again!*)
- Did Job pretend it was no big deal? (*No way! He tore his clothes and shaved his head. These were the ultimate signs of sadness in his culture.*)
- What action did Job take? (*He prayed and worshiped God.*)
- What attitude did Job have? (*He realized God knew what He was doing.*)

Transition to the next step by stating that even if things in our lives are as stressful as what Job was facing, we can rely on God to care for us and be with us. As we read in 1 Peter 5:7, we can "cast all [our] anxiety on him because he cares for [us]."

Option 2: Body Language. For this option, you will need several Bibles.

Begin by explaining that "body language" is the way we communicate our feelings through our facial expressions and/or the way we position our bodies. It communicates a ton of unspoken feelings—often more than words themselves can relate. To illustrate this, strike a few different poses and have the group members guess what you're communicating. (Try expressing the following emotions: boredom, impatience, anger, fear, joy and superiority.)

Continue by stating that all of us are faced with situations that cause us stress. When these times come, there is really only one type of body language we should adopt. Get down on your knees (yes, literally) and share that during stressful times, we need to go to our knees in worship! God wants us to bring our problems and stresses to Him. Sometimes He will immediately take those problems away, but sometimes He will allow us to remain in that situation for some time. Regardless, it is important to remember that God has not forgotten us—He is doing something good through the situation. God is always right there with us in the middle of our stress, and He will help us get through it.

Distribute the Bibles and explain that prayer is an awesome thing. We can "go to our knees" in prayer at any time and take our requests to God! Choose a volunteer to read Philippians 4:4-7. State that this passage tells us some important things about how we should handle fear and anxiety:

- We should rejoice in the Lord always (see verse 4).
- We should not be anxious about anything (see verse 6).
- In every situation, we should present our requests to God and give Him thanks (see verse 6).
- When we do, "the peace of God, which transcends all understanding, will guard our hearts and our minds in Christ Jesus" (see verse 7).

Explain that God is telling us we don't need to worry because He can handle our problems. He has everything under control, and we can trust Him. This is the attitude we need to have. Ask the group members how a person's body language while he or she is praying might show that the person is giving God control of his or her stressful situation. (Some answers could be kneeling down or raising his or her hands.)

Transition to the next step by stating that we can trust God even in the midst of incredibly stressful situations. God knows the pressures that we are under, and He is there to give us His peace when we ask. He is always at work in our lives.

DIG

Option 1: Name that Stressor. For this option, you will need a whiteboard, a whiteboard marker, paper and pens or pencils.

Divide the students into groups of three to five people. Distribute the paper and pens or pencils and ask the groups to pick one person who will write down the group's answers. Have each group list as many things as they can that can cause stress for young people today. Allow them three to five minutes to do this, and when the groups are finished, invite them to share their lists. As they share, write down their ideas on the whiteboard.

When they are finished, ask the group members to discuss how a person might be able to fight against the stress that each situation causes. Explain that our first action should always be to go to God with the problem, for He is the one who can help us. As we do our part and allow God to intervene into the situation, we can effectively fight back against stress.

Option 2: Big Ball of Stress. For this option, you will need just this book. Share the following case study with the group:

> Brad is a big ball of stress. He just can't seem to shake it! At night, he stresses about getting his homework done and what he will wear to school the next day. During the day, he worries about getting good grades, being accepted by his teachers and classmates, and not saying anything stupid in class. To top it off, Brad stresses about being short! His youth leader told him to pray about his stress, but that doesn't seem like much of a solution to Brad.

Discuss the following questions with the group:

- What is the main cause of Brad's stress? (*Brad himself! He is insecure and worries about meeting the expectations and standards of others.*)

- Can Brad ever totally be free of stress? (*Not completely. Life is full of things that can stress us out—which is what makes it challenging. The key for Brad is to stop doing things that add to his stress level.*)

- What things could Brad do to get rid of some of his stress? (*He could talk to God about the things that make him worry. He could set aside enough time to get his homework done. He could show respect to his teachers and earn their respect by simply doing his best in their classes.*)

APPLY

Option 1: My Stress Prayer. For this option, you will need copies of "My Stress Prayer" (found on the next page) and pens or pencils.

Begin by dividing the group members into teams of three to five people and distribute "My Stress Prayer" and pens or pencils. Instruct the group members to write down one area of stress in their lives. Have each person share his or her area of stress with the group, and then ask the groups to come up with

My Stress Prayer

What is currently stressing you out at school?

_____
_____
_____
_____
_____

Here are five things the group came up with that I could do to reduce this stress:

1. _____
2. _____
3. _____
4. _____
5. _____

In the space below, write a prayer to God and ask Him to help you handle this pressure-packed situation.

Dear God,

_____
_____
_____
_____
_____
_____

Amen.

five things that the person could do to reduce this stress and pressure in his or her life.

Give the groups 10 minutes to work through the items on the handout. When everyone is finished, close your time together in prayer. Conclude by sharing your own prayer to God about an area of stress in your own life. Extend an invitation for students to share what they have written on their handouts, and then pray for those specific needs.

Option 2: Stress in the Bible. For this option, you will need several Bibles, a whiteboard, a whiteboard marker, paper and pens or pencils.

Ahead of time, write the names of the following Bible characters and the accompanying Scripture references on the whiteboard: Abraham (Genesis 22:1-14), Moses' mom (Exodus 1:22–2:4), Ruth (Ruth 1), Hannah (1 Samuel 1:1-17) and Josiah (2 Kings 22:1–23:3).

Divide the students into groups of three to five people. Distribute Bibles, paper and pens or pencils. Point out what you have written on the whiteboard and explain that the Bible provides us with some real-life case studies of stressful challenges and situations. Ask the groups to look up the passages and then write down their answers to these questions:

- What stressful situation(s) did the person face?
- How did that character handle the stress?
- Did that character handle the stress well? Why or why not?

Give the groups a few minutes to work on the verses, and then briefly discuss each group's findings. Close by instructing the group members to share one thing they can do differently when they feel stressed out this week. Ask everyone in the small groups to pray for that person and the situation that he or she is facing.

Youth Leader Tip
Note that what stresses out group members will differ. Some may find running a mile during class stressful, while others will relish the chance to show off—both in gym class and in your youth group!

REFLECT

The following short devotions are for the group members to reflect on and answer during the week. You can make a copy of these pages and distribute to your class or download and print from **www.gospellight.com/uncommon/jh_ dealing_with_pressure.zip.**

1—DON'T FRET

Flip open your Bible to about the middle and read Psalm 37:7-8. According to this passage, what is the biggest problem with "fretting" (stressing out)?

- ❏ It can give you a stomachache and a headache.
- ❏ It will keep you awake at night.
- ❏ It can lead to evil and keep you from trusting God.
- ❏ It can make you hungry and lead you to snack chips and cookies.

Although the first, second and fourth answers might be problems, the biggest problem with stress is that it keeps you from trusting God. As the psalmist warns, fretting "leads only to evil." It's ultimately a message that you don't trust God and believe He's in control.

Read Proverbs 3:5-6. According to these verses, what is the opposite of stressing out when under pressure?

_____

_____

_____

_____

What do these verses say will happen if you trust God?

_____

_____

_____

_____

When you trust God, He will "make your paths straight." This means He will lead you and help you with the thing you are worried about! So spend a few minutes talking to God and tell Him your problem. Ask Him for His help. He is listening!

2—WORRYWARTS

To read about a true pressure situation, turn to John 6:1-15.

In this story, we read that a great crowd of people had come to hear Jesus speak. At one point, Jesus decided to test His disciples by asking them where they would buy bread to feed all the people. The crowd was hungry, and there was no way to get food to them. There were no restaurants or drive-thrus—they were out in the middle of nowhere.

How did Philip answer Jesus' question? How did Andrew respond?

_____

_____

_____

How did Jesus ultimately fix the problem?

_____

_____

_____

Think about what is causing you stress today. If Jesus could feed more than 5,000 people with just two fish and five loaves (buns, really) of bread, what do you think He could do for you? Picture in your mind how God could take care of your situation if you would only trust Him.

3—WHEN THE HEAT RISES

Is it getting hot in here? Turn to the story of Daniel's three friends told in Daniel 3:1-30. Which of the following would cause you the most pressure and stress if it happened to you today at school?

- ❏ Spilling a drink in your lap that left an embarrassing wet stain.
- ❏ Slipping on wet grass and falling into a puddle.
- ❏ Having a friend you've known since fourth grade make fun of you for something you did.
- ❏ Realizing that you have a major test today in history—and you completely forgot about it.
- ❏ Doing something really embarrassing in front the person you have a crush on.

None of those situations would be fun, but you have to agree they wouldn't be as bad as what Shadrach, Meshach and Abednego were facing. These three men had been commanded to worship a golden image of King Nebuchadnezzar, but they refused to do so because they worshiped only the one true God. These men trusted God completely. They knew the Lord could save them—but even if He didn't, they would still trust Him. That's a pretty good way to get rid of stress.

Is it hard for you to trust God in every situation? Why?

_____

_____

_____

Spend some time praying today about something that is stressing you out. Remember that if God can save three guys from a fire, He can handle whatever you're going through, too.

4—WHAT IF?

What does Jesus say about worry? Read Luke 12:22-31 to find out.

Hali was the biggest "what if" worrier in the whole school. She was always stressed out about something. What if Mr. Reynolds gives us a pop quiz in math? What if the cafeteria runs out of those chicken sandwiches I like at lunch? What if Troy doesn't call me back? What if the school runs out of yearbooks before I can get one? On and on it went.

The problem with asking "what if?" all the time is that it makes you worry about things that are completely out of your control. Soon, you will be completely overwhelmed with pressures. God doesn't want you live that way. He wants you to turn to Him when you have worries and trust in Him for the answer.

What three things does Jesus tell us not to worry about in Luke 12:22?

_____

_____

_____

When you start to worry about something today, do the following. First, think about Jesus as quickly as you can. Next, let go of your worries—give your concerns to Him and tell Him you want Him to take them. Keep thinking about Jesus until all the "what ifs" are gone and you feel God's peace coming over you.

THE PRESSURE OF TEACHERS

THE BIG IDEA
Teachers aren't perfect, but God still wants us to respect them, obey them and show them His love.

SESSION AIMS
In this session, you will guide group members to (1) learn that their teachers have struggles outside of the classroom; (2) understand how to express their feelings when they encounter particularly tough teachers at school; and (3) choose to obey God by showing respect to their teachers.

THE BIGGEST VERSE
"Everyone must submit himself to the governing authorities, for there is no authority except that which God has established. The authorities that exist have been established by God" (Romans 13:1).

OTHER IMPORTANT VERSES
1 Samuel 24; Jeremiah 29:11; John 3:16; Romans 8:28; 12:17-21; 13:1-5; 1 Corinthians 13:1-8; Ephesians 4:29; Philippians 2:3-8; Colossians 4:5-6; 1 Thessalonians 5:12-13; 1 Timothy 4:12,15-16; 5:1-2; 1 John 4:10

Note: Additional options and worksheets in 8^1/$_2$" x 11" format for this session are available for download at **www.gospellight.com/uncommon/jh_dealing_with_pressure.zip**.

STARTER

Option 1: Get Moving. For this option, you will need just this book.

Greet the group members and explain that you will be reading a list of commands that they are to follow. If a command calls for them to move to a chair in front of them and they are in the front row, they need to move behind all of the rows of chairs and continue playing from there. Likewise, if they are told to move backward and they are in the last row, they must move to the front of the rows of chairs. If the instruction is to move to the right and they are in last seat on the right end of the row, they must move to the left end of the row; and if they are told to move to the left and they are in last seat on the left end of the row, they must move to the right end of the row. Get the picture?

Read through the commands quickly. There are no winners or losers in this game—the purpose is just the get the group members out of their seats and moving. Here are the commands that you will give to your group:

- Stand up if you take gym class.
- Do three jumping jacks if you look forward to gym class every day.
- Move two plus two chairs to the right if you think you're good at math.
- Move eight divided by two chairs ahead if you think you stink at math.
- Raise your right hand if you can spell the word "receipt." (*Choose one person to spell it out loud, but don't tell him or her if the spelling is correct.*)
- If you think that is the correct way to spell "receipt," put your left arm in the air. (*Now either give the correct spelling or affirm that the person was correct.*)
- If you were correct, sit on the floor in front of your chair. If you were wrong, jog two laps around the room. (*Move ahead with the game and let any joggers join in when they've finished their laps.*)
- If lunch is your favorite time during the school day, stand up and turn in a circle five times, counting aloud. (*If they don't count loud enough or enthusiastically enough, make them do it again!*)
- (*Ask one of the twirling students*): What is your favorite school lunch menu item?
- If this is also your favorite lunch item, hop up and down on one foot 10 times and count the hops so I can hear you.
- If you know the answer to this next question, look at the ceiling: Who was the president of the United States in 1862? (*Again, choose one person with a raised head to answer. Do not give the answer or tell the group whether or not this is correct yet.*)

- If you think this answer is wrong, look at your shoes. If you think it is right, keep looking at the ceiling. (*Once everyone has voted, state that the correct answer is Abraham Lincoln. Have the group members who were wrong do 10 push-ups.*)
- Hop from one foot to the other if you know the answer to this question: What is the normal body temperature of a human being? (*Choose a volunteer to respond, but before he or she shares the answer, tell the group that if this person gets the answer right, everyone can sit down. However, if the person gets the answer wrong, everyone must do 20 jumping jacks and then jog two laps around the room. Now get the volunteer's answer and follow through on the appropriate consequences. The correct answer is 98.6 degrees Fahrenheit.*)

Once the group members have returned to their seats and have settled down, discuss the following questions:

- Were any of you afraid to answer a question because of the possible consequences? (*The answer will likely be yes, because they could have been the only one who got the question wrong, which would have been embarrassing.*)
- Are you ever afraid to answer questions during a class at school? (*Most of us have been at one time or another!*)
- Why are you afraid? What do you think will happen? (*Allow students to respond.*)

Explain that while they won't be twirling and running around their classroom at school, they do have to answer questions every day. Guess what? So do their teachers. It's tiring for them as well. Today, the group is going to try to understand what it's like to be a teacher and learn how God wants us to treat them.

Option 2: Course Concept Cards. For this option, you will need the following items for every 8 to 10 students: an adult volunteer, a flipchart, an easel, a marker, and a copy of "Course Concept Cards" (found on the next page). You will also need a prize for the winning team and a whistle, cowbell or something else to use as a signal that can be heard over the noise of teens shouting out their answers.

Ahead of time, set up a flipchart placed on an easel with one marker for each team. Copy and cut the handouts into cards. Stack one set of cards for

COURSE CONCEPT CARDS

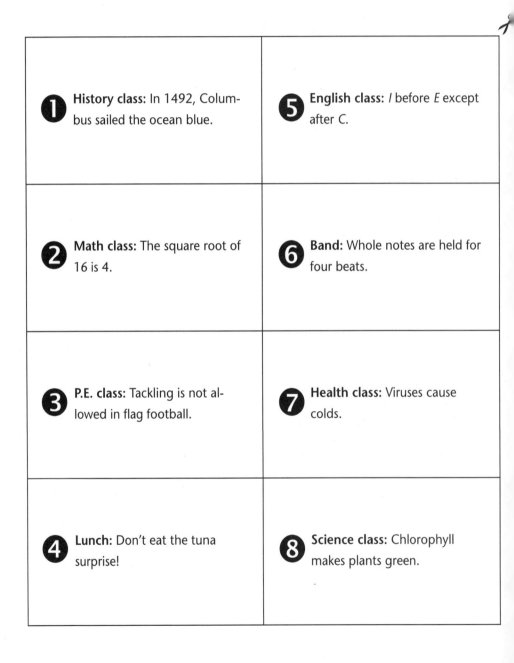

① History class: In 1492, Columbus sailed the ocean blue.

② Math class: The square root of 16 is 4.

③ P.E. class: Tackling is not allowed in flag football.

④ Lunch: Don't eat the tuna surprise!

⑤ English class: *I* before *E* except after *C*.

⑥ Band: Whole notes are held for four beats.

⑦ Health class: Viruses cause colds.

⑧ Science class: Chlorophyll makes plants green.

each team in numerical order, with card number 1 on top. Have one adult volunteer standing by at each station to assist and help out if the teams get stuck.

Greet the group members and divide them into teams of 8 to 10 people. Send each team to a station. Have the group members line up a few feet away from their team's flipchart. Instruct the adult leaders to hold the stack of cards, making sure the cards stay in their proper order and that the group members only see the top card.

Next, tell the teams that at your signal, the first player will need to run to his or her team's flipchart, look at the top concept card, and begin drawing what he or she thinks will help his or her team guess the concept. There are a few simple rules:

- The person drawing cannot speak or make any hand gestures.
- The person drawing cannot write any words or numbers on the flipchart.
- If the person drawing cannot figure out what to draw, he or she can allow the next player in line to take a turn by running back and tagging that person. Each team is only allowed two passes during the game.

Note that some of the phrases on these cards will likely be tough for the group members to draw and/or guess. That's okay! The frustration will (hopefully) help them relate to how teachers sometimes feel when they're trying to teach a class.

When the game begins and the person begins drawing, the rest of the team must yell out what they think is being drawn. When a team correctly guesses a concept, that team's adult leader should award them 10 points and wave at you so you can sound the signal to end that round. When the signal is sounded, the player who is drawing must put down the marker, run back to his or her line, and tag the player for the next round. Give the teams two or three minutes to guess each answer. If no team guesses correctly in that time, sound the signal and have them move to the next round.

After all eight rounds are finished, tally up the points and award a prize to the winning team. Have the group members sit down with their teams as you discuss the following questions:

- Which concept was the hardest to draw?
- How did you feel when it was your turn to draw?
- How did you feel when you heard the signal to stop before your team guessed the answer?

- Why do you think that trying to get a group of junior-highers to understand what you are showing them might be similar to what your
  teachers go through every day?

Explain that today the group is going to learn what the Bible says about
how they are to treat people at school—including their teachers. The group just
might be in for some surprises!

MESSAGE

Option 1: David and Saul Roleplay. For this option, you will need several
Bibles, paper and pens or pencils.

Begin by asking the group members to describe how they think they treat
their teachers. Now ask how they think God would want them to treat their
teachers. Explain that while the Bible actually doesn't mention much about
teachers in particular, it does talk about *submission* to *authority*, which does apply to teachers. This is because their teachers have been placed in a position of
authority over them.

Choose a volunteer to read Romans 13:1-5.[1] Following this, discuss these
questions as a group:

- Paul never says to obey the authority that is over us, but he does say to
  submit to it. What is the difference? (*Although Paul says we should submit to those in authority, he is allowing for the possibility that the authority might be asking us to do something that goes against what God would
  want, in which case we would not need to obey. A good example of this is
  found in Acts 5:29, where the apostles were ordered to stop preaching the
  gospel but replied, "We must obey God rather than men!"*)
- According to these verses, who has established the authorities that exist? (*God.*)
- In what way are our teachers God's servants who are there for our own
  good? (*They are trying to teach us things we need to know.*)
- According to Paul, why are we supposed to submit to authority? (*We
  are to submit because if we don't, there will be consequences. Furthermore,
  if we don't submit, it will go against our consciences, and we will know that
  we are doing the wrong thing.*)
- Can you give some examples of experiences at school where you didn't
  submit? What happened? (*Allow students to respond.*)

Because these concepts are abstract, you might want to use the following Old Testament narrative to make the ideas more tangible and accessible. Explain that we might often view teachers as enemies because they make our lives difficult. In the Bible, there was a young man named David who had the same problem. A king named Saul was in authority over David, and the worst part was that the king was trying to kill David! Ask the group members how anyone could possibly submit to someone like that in this situation. Well, we are about to learn how David did it.

Choose 10 volunteers to assist you in portraying the story of David. Assign the following roles: King Saul, a messenger, David, 3,000 men (three of the largest volunteers) and David's men (four volunteers). In your best game-show announcer's voice, introduce the story as follows:

Now, sit back, relax and prepare to be wowed by today's scintillating story of a mad king named Saul, a friendship gone *really* bad, and a future king on the run for his life! As you may remember from the Old Testament, God chose a young lad named David to be king of Israel someday. But first David had a lot of growing up to do. David actually began his career as king-to-be by playing his harp for King Saul. A short time later, armed with only a slingshot and a small stone, David killed a giant named Goliath who was terrorizing King Saul's great army! After that, Saul took a liking to David, and he asked him to come live with him in the royal palace. As David grew older and stronger, he helped the kings defeat many of Israel's foes. Pretty soon, people were writing songs about David and proclaiming how much better he was than the king. Well, old Saul became green with envy about that, so he tried to hunt David down and kill him!

Instruct the actors to begin their role-play as you read 1 Samuel 24. They should act out whatever you are saying and repeat any spoken dialogue after you've read it. For longer passages, they can just move their lips as you read. When the performance has ended, discuss the following questions:

- Do you think Saul was David's enemy? (*In David's eyes, Saul was not his enemy. Even though Saul was trying to harm him, David chose to think of Saul not as his adversary but as his king.*)
- What did David's buddies tell him to do? (*They encouraged David to kill Saul while there was an opportunity to do so.*)

- Why didn't David take this opportunity to kill Saul? (*David respected Saul's God-given position as king, so he refused to do anything to harm him.*)
- How does David's story help us understand what Paul wrote in Romans 13:1-5? (*Even when we have disagreements or struggles with those in authority over us, we can still choose to honor their position and can seek to resolve problems with respect.*)
- Do you feel that some of your teachers are against you? (*Allow students to answer.*)
- Why do you feel this way? What do your teachers do? (*Some answers might including assigning difficult homework, giving hard tests, requiring excellence in work, and so on.*)
- If David were to walk into this room and give you some advice about how to handle these things, what do you think he would say? (*God has placed teachers in authority over our lives to help direct and instruct us. When we choose to respect their positions of authority, God will bless us and cause us to succeed.*)
- What might Paul say about your teachers if he walked into this room right now? (*God can use any authority He has placed on earth to bring about good. However, sometimes those in authority are corrupt and will expect us to do things we know are wrong. Remember that the ultimate authority is God Himself. As we submit to His authority, He will help us deal with the other authority figures in our lives.*)
- How is this advice different from the way we tend to act? (*We are sometimes encouraged to fight against the authority of our teachers instead of respectfully submit to it. However, having people in authority over us is part of God's plan for our lives. It was His idea. We should try to follow those in authority, unless they are asking us to directly disobey God's Word.*)

To bring this idea home, suggest several situations in which students must choose to submit to the authority over them, even though they may not like what they're being asked to do. Here are a few examples:

- A teacher assigns homework over the holiday break. Do you blow it off because you don't like doing homework during vacation, or do you decide to keep a good attitude and do your best on the assignment?
- The principal decides to close down the lunchtime Bible club. Do you stop meeting altogether and plot revenge, or do you find another time and place to meet, pray and read God's Word?

- Your teacher decides the class should stay in during a break to clean up the mess they made doing a special project. Do you rebel and walk out as soon as the bell rings, or do you give up a few minutes of your break to do what you've been asked to do?

The idea is to help your group members understand that submission is a choice they must make and that most authorities in their lives are good for them in one way or another.

Option 2: Another Person's Shoes. For this option, you will need your Bible, a whiteboard and a whiteboard marker.

Begin by reading Romans 13:1-5. Explain that in this passage, Paul shows us how we are to treat those who have been placed in authority over us—including teachers! Teachers are "God's servants," and He has placed them in our lives to give us the tools we need to succeed in the present and in the future. However, that doesn't always mean that it will be easy to get along with our teachers.

Remind the group that teachers are *real people* who have their own set of problems, bad moods and bad hair days. In fact, there is an old saying that states, "Don't judge a man until you've walked a mile in his shoes." That's good advice, so ask the group members to take off their shoes and to throw them into a pile in the middle of the room. When you say "go," they will go back to the pile, find a pair of shoes (matching or not), put them on their feet and return to their seats.

When this exercise is complete, discuss the following questions:

- How does it feel to wear another person's shoes?
- Are the shoes you are wearing too tight? Too loose?
- Are the shoes a style you would buy if you saw them in a store? Why or why not?

Explain that sometimes, their parents, friends and even their teachers will treat them badly, and their immediate reaction will be to react in a negative way. However, it's important to try to determine *why* the person is acting that way. Maybe their teacher's car broke down on the way to school and he or she missed the first two classes because of it. Maybe the teacher just lost a parent to cancer. Maybe the teacher has a headache but came to school anyway because the school couldn't find a substitute.

Ask the group members to think of a time when they had a bad day and took it out on their parents or friends. In the same way, before they assume that a teacher is mean or hates them, they should try to understand what that person might be going through at the time. Remind the group that in Ephesians 4:32, Paul says, "Be kind and compassionate to one another, forgiving each other, just as in Christ God forgave you."

Conclude by asking the group members to spend a few minutes talking to God about how their teachers make them mad or upset. Also have them ask God to help them respond to those difficult teachers in a respectful and loving way, and have them pray for any specific needs or problems their teachers might be having. Remind the group that it is almost impossible to stay mad at someone when you are praying for him or her!

DIG

Option 1: Understanding Your Teachers. For this option, you will need several Bibles, copies of "Understanding Your Teachers" (found on the next page), pens or pencils and a prize.

Divide the students into groups of five to seven people and distribute copies of "Understanding Your Teachers" and pens or pencils. Explain that the groups will look up each of the passages on the handout and then write down one way each verse can help them to better understand and treat their teachers. Let the groups know that the team that comes up with the most creative idea will win a prize. (Note: For time consideration, you can also just assign one or two verses to each group.)

After several minutes, ask the groups to take turns sharing their ideas. Give a prize to the group that has the most creative idea.

Option 2: The Substitute. For this option, you will need just this case study. Read the following aloud to your group:

> Erin sat down at her desk at the back of her English class. She liked this class the most because she got to sit between her two best friends, Jessica and Andrea.
>
> When Jessica arrived, she leaned over to Erin and whispered, "Did you hear that we have a sub for the rest of the semester?"
>
> "Yeah," said Andrea, "Mrs. Stevens had her baby this weekend. She's on maternity leave."

Understanding Your Teachers

Use the following verses to come up with ideas regarding how to better understand and treat your teachers:

Romans 12:17-21

_____
_____
_____

Ephesians 4:29

_____
_____
_____

Philippians 2:3-8

_____
_____
_____

1 Timothy 4:12,15-16

_____
_____
_____

1 Timothy 5:1-2

_____
_____
_____

"Wow. Who's going to be our sub?" Erin asked.

"I heard it's old Mrs. MacIntosh," said Andrea. "She was a sub in my science class, and she didn't like me at all!"

"I heard she changes the seating chart so friends can't sit together," Jessica said.

"I think I had her in history one time," said Erin. "She *was* kind of mean."

"Well, we'll show her," said Andrea. "Brett has a plan to make Mrs. MacIntosh wish she'd never agreed to sub!" She chuckled.

"What do you mean?" Erin asked.

"You'll see. Just watch Brett and do whatever he does," said Andrea. "If we all do it, then none of us can get in trouble."

Discuss the following questions:

- What would you do if you were Erin?
- If you found out that Brett's prank was harmless, would you go along with the rest of the class?
- What other explanation might there be for the way Mrs. MacIntosh has acted in her other classes?
- What have you learned today that might help you make the best choice?

Transition to the next step by reminding the group that in Romans 12:17, Paul says, "Do not repay anyone evil for evil. Be careful to do what is right in the eyes of everybody." If we want to serve God and love others, we need to make sure that we are not taking part in anything that will cause harm or disrespect—even if the prank seems innocent.

APPLY

Option 1: A Letter to Me. For this option, you will need stationary or lined paper, business-sized envelopes, and pens or pencils.

Distribute the paper, envelopes and pens or pencils. Explain to the group members that for the next couple of minutes, they will be writing a letter to themselves. In this letter, they will include three ways they plan to show more respect to their least favorite teachers at school. Tell them that if they're having trouble thinking of ideas, they can ask you or get suggestions from each other.

Allow a few minutes for the letter writing. When the group members are finished, have them place their letters in their envelopes, seal the envelopes and address them with their names and addresses. Collect the letters from the students and tell them that you will be mailing them out sometime during the next couple of weeks. (Make sure you do it!) When they receive these letters, they will serve as reminders for them to continue to be respectful to their teachers.

Option 2: Showing God's Love. For this option, you will need a whiteboard and a whiteboard marker. In addition, depending on which option you choose below, you will need construction paper, scissors, glue, glitter, markers, stickers and laminating paper or a laminating machine to create bookmarks or cards.

Explain to the group that it's one thing to show someone respect but a different thing entirely to show him or her God's love. Ask the group members to brainstorm some ways they could show their teachers that God loves them. Use the whiteboard to write down their suggestions. When you are finished, discuss ways you can put those ideas into action, or use one of the following suggestions:

- Create a bookmark for their teachers with a word of encouragement and a Bible verse about God's love. You will need to provide some sample verses for the group members to get them started, such as Jeremiah 29:11, John 3:16 or 1 John 4:10. This idea will not fly with every group, so decide if it is a good plan for your particular mix of individuals.
- Write a letter of encouragement to their teachers. The group members could point out something positive about each person's teaching style or something unique about the class itself.
- Pool resources and buy some remembrances to give their teachers. Some items might include candy, flowers, pens, and so on.
- As a group, invite the teachers to attend a special church event—an upcoming holiday concert, play, banquet and so forth. These types of events would be easier for students to promote than a church service.

Challenge your group to put these or the ideas they brainstormed into action—and do it soon! Making it a group project might get a better response. Keep a written record of the ideas they chose, and be sure to check back with them each week to find out the progress they have made. Also ask the students to share their stories, as hearing about their peers' successes will help others have the courage to act as well.

Wrap up by asking a few group members to pray for the teachers in their schools. Also pray that they will show these adults in authority greater respect by showing them God's love.

REFLECT

The following short devotions are for the group members to reflect on and answer during the week. You can make a copy of these pages and distribute to your class or download and print from **www.gospellight.com/uncommon/jh_ dealing_with_pressure.zip.**

1—SHOW SOME RESPECT

Happy, happy, joy, joy! Go read Hebrews 13:17!

Jane Kindly was the science teacher at Fairly Middle School. Her job was a lot harder than it looked—she taught seven classes every day and never the same thing for more than one class! During one period she taught chemistry; in another she taught about the solar system; and in the next she would taught about the environment. She spent a lot of time preparing for each class, grading papers and thinking about her students.

Some of her classes were really fun to teach and had respectful students who, even though they didn't know all the answers, tried hard to learn what she was teaching. Other classes were hard for her to teach. The students were rude to her and spent a lot of time making smart remarks and pulling practical jokes. Often she was sad and tired at the end of the day.

Sometimes it's easy to forget that your teachers are real people too. They have friends, families, stresses, problems and lives just like anybody else. According to Hebrews 13:17, how should you treat your teachers?

_____

_____

_____

What is one thing you can do to help your teachers find joy in their work today?

_____

_____

_____

2—*PI* AND YOU

Read Matthew 10:24 to see what Jesus had to say about teachers.

Imagine you're in math class studying *pi* when—*blam!*—you are able to read your classmates' minds! Which of these students has the best attitude?

❏ Jessica Platt: *This class is so boring. This teacher stinks. Why does he have to wear that stupid sweater all the time?*

❏ Henry James: Pi. *What a dumb name for a bunch of numbers. I bet the teacher made it up. He would do something like that just to make himself look smarter than the rest of us.*

❏ Tamar DeFoe: *Man, this stuff is kind of dry, but I'd better pay attention. The teacher wouldn't spend all this time on it if it wasn't important.*

❏ Kevin Ham: *Mmm . . . pie really sounds good. I wonder what my mom put in my lunch?*

Do you feel your thoughts are respectful or disrespectful to your teachers?

_____

_____

_____

If you are guilty of being disrespectful, what can you do to change? (An example would be paying attention to what that teacher is saying.)

_____

_____

_____

Today, ask God to help you show more respect to each of your teachers.

3—DON'T LET GO!

Grab Proverbs 4:13 and don't let go!

Jess had trouble paying attention in her math class. It was her last class of the day, and she always gazed out the window instead of listening to her teacher. She barely passed the class with a C-, but she didn't care. "It's just a dumb math class," she told her friend Gina. "Who needs that junk anyway?"

Jess was excited, because she was going to a science camp that summer. She loved mixing chemicals together and looking through telescopes. Imagine how lost she felt when she realized they would be using mathematical calculations to figure out how much of one chemical to mix with another, or where Mars was located in the night sky. If only she had paid attention in her "dumb" math class.

Jess didn't think learning math was important, so she blew it off and didn't take the class or the instructor very seriously at all. But it caught up to her, and she regretted how she had behaved.

The writer of Proverbs 4:13 states how we should feel about instruction (education, teachers and classes). Below, write out this verse as if you were speaking it directly to Jess in the story above.

_____

_____

_____

Today, pray that God will help you learn some new things that will help you serve Him better.

4—THAT WASN'T FUNNY

Hey, you! Yeah, you! Get to Proverbs 13:13 as quickly as you can.

Scott Hansen set off a stink bomb in Ms. Ivors's history class. Everyone ran out of the classroom and into the hall because of the smell, where they laughed and congratulated Scott on his prank. Ms. Ivors, however, didn't think it was so funny and sent Scott to the principal. At lunch, a few of the kids got together and talked about it. With which of their opinions do you agree?

- ☐ "Scott was just trying to be funny. Ms. Ivors has no sense of humor."
- ☐ "That smell was horrible, but it did get us out of class."
- ☐ "Scott is totally immature, but Ms. Ivors is a jerk. It was just a joke."
- ☐ "That prank was weak. I mean, Ms. Ivors has a job to do, and Scott is not helping by lighting off stink bombs in class."

Does your response agree with or go against Proverbs 13:13? Why or why not?

_____

_____

_____

If your response was to go against the teacher, according to Proverbs 13:13, what might the consequence be for you?

_____

_____

_____

If you have been scorning instruction instead of respecting your teacher's commands, today ask God to turn your situation around.

THE PRESSURE OF BEING DIFFERENT

THE BIG IDEA

When we live by the Spirit, we will act differently than others do in the world around us.

SESSION AIMS

In this session, you will guide group members to (1) understand that Christians should act differently than nonbelievers; (2) learn how to deal with the feelings that come from not always fitting in and from being different; and (3) come up with a plan to deal with the pressures that these differences bring.

THE BIGGEST VERSE

"They admitted that they were aliens and strangers on earth" (Hebrews 11:13).

OTHER IMPORTANT VERSES

Exodus 34:29-35; Luke 6:27-31; John 1:12; 9:13-34; 1 Corinthians 4:6-7; Galatians 5:16-26; Ephesians 5:8; Hebrews 11:14-16; 1 Peter 2:11-12

Note: Additional options and worksheets in 8¹/₂" x 11" format for this session are available for download at **www.gospellight.com/uncommon/jh_dealing_with_pressure.zip**.

STARTER

Option 1: Aliens Have Landed. For this option, you will need a whiteboard and a whiteboard marker (or another way to list the five "customs" so the group members can remember them). Greet the students and divide them into an even number of groups from 3 to 12 people. Explain that each group represents a spaceship of aliens from a different planet that has just landed on earth.

State that each group will need to choose a name for its home planet. In addition, the group will need to decide how its "culture" performs each of the following customs that you are going to list on the whiteboard:

1. How the beings greet one another (on earth it is a handshake).
2. How the beings say "hello."
3. Three things that offend the beings on your planet (these should be things that people on earth do all the time, especially just after meeting another person).
4. The acceptable way to sit on your planet.
5. How the beings on your planet respond when someone asks them a question.

Allow three to five minutes for the groups to figure out their planet's names and customs. When the groups are ready, ask them to first give their planet's name, and then write each name on the whiteboard. Next, announce to the group members which planet will visit another planet. Using the customs they have listed, have the groups from the planets visit for three minutes, and then switch the groups. Do this two or three times, depending on the number of groups and the amount time you have.

When you are finished, have everyone return to their seats. Discuss the following questions as a group:

- Which planet had the strangest customs?
- Which planet seemed to be the most like earth?
- Have you ever been in another country and found the rules and the behavior of its people to be different from that with which you were familiar? (*If anyone has, invite him or her to describe what was different.*)

Transition to the next step by explaining that although we as Christians are (hopefully) not as strange as some of the alien groups we have seen here today, sometimes the choices we make might make us seem different from our friends.

Option 2: Hop to It. For this option, you will need a small prize that the winning team can share. There are a couple of ways you can play this game depending on the size of your group, as follows:

- Small group (1 to 6 students): The group members can spread out across the room and play the game individually.

- Medium group (7 to 15 students): Divide the main group into two teams that will compete against each other.

- Large group (16 or more students): Divide the main group into multiple teams that will compete against each other.

Regardless of how you choose to play the game, the group members will need to decide whether the statements you tell them are *true* or *false*. State that when they believe a statement is true, they should hop to the right. When they believe a statement is false, they should hop to the left. The statements that you will read are about certain behaviors in other cultures, as follows:

- In Argentina, it's polite to greet people, even strangers, by kissing them on the cheek. (*True.*)
- In Iceland, you would be considered rude if you happened to sneeze on someone. (*True.*)
- People from the South Pacific island of Tangano pinch each other's cheeks to say hello. (*False. There's no such island!*)
- In some Middle Eastern countries, you give the cook a compliment by belching after a big meal. (*True.*)
- When people from Greenland say, "Your hair is showing," it really means, "Stop making a fool of yourself." (*False.*)
- In England, people hold their fork in their left hand and their knife in their right hand while eating. (*True.*)

Youth Leader Tip

It happens almost every time a game comes up: a few students do not want to play. How do you handle this? While you never want to force anyone to play, you can require that they at least stand or sit with their team.

- In the Bahamas, it is not considered appropriate to go to the beach on Sunday. (*True.*)
- Tiberian women never speak in public. (*False.*)
- In Zimbabwe, it's considered impolite to smile at someone you don't know. (*False.*)
- In Denmark and Holland, French fries are served with mayonnaise, not ketchup. (*True.*)
- Russian men greet each other with a big ol' kiss on the lips. (*True.*)
- In most countries other than the United States, you would never ask to use the restroom or bathroom—you would ask for the "toilet." (*True.*)

If you are working with teams, give them 30 seconds to decide their answers before hopping together. Award 100 points for each correct answer. (Note: If your country is given in this list, substitute your country's statement with the following: "People in the United States are often seen by other cultures as being loud, rude and obnoxious." *True.*)

Award prizes to the team with the most points. Transition to the next step by explaining that each day we are required to make choices about how we will act, and sometimes others will form an opinion of us based on those choices. For this reason, we need to make the *right* choices for God—even if it makes us stand out in a crowd or appear different from others.

MESSAGE

Option 1: Alien Questionnaire. For this option, you need several Bibles, copies of "Alien Questionnaire" (found on the next page), pens or pencils and two to six adult volunteers who are familiar with the biblical figures from Hebrews 11.

Ahead of time, assign each adult volunteer a role as one of the Old Testament heroes of the faith mentioned in Hebrews 11. There are 16 individuals mentioned specifically by name: Abel, Enoch, Noah, Abraham, Isaac, Jacob, Esau, Joseph, Moses, Rahab, Gideon, Barak, Samson, Jephthah, David and Samuel. The volunteers should study the entire Hebrews 11 passage and be prepared to answer the interview questions listed on the handout.[1] (You might also want to provide them with the information that is given in the other two options for this section.)

Distribute a copy of the "Alien Questionnaire" and pens or pencils to each person in the group. Introduce each adult volunteer by the name of the character who they will be portraying. For example, you could say, "Can you believe

 # ALIEN QUESTIONNAIRE

BIBLE CHARACTER #1: _____

Why did you feel like you were an alien and a stranger?

_____
_____
_____
_____

How did the way you felt about yourself affect your actions?

_____
_____
_____

How did other people treat you?

_____
_____
_____

BIBLE CHARACTER #2: _____

Why did you feel like you were an alien and a stranger?

_____
_____
_____
_____

How did the way you felt about yourself affect your actions?

_____
_____
_____

How did other people treat you?

_____
_____
_____

it? Moses decided to join our group tonight! And over there, I'd like you to meet Abraham!" Ham it up! Ask the group members to work in pairs or trios. Using the questions on the handouts, each group will need to move around the room, interview two of the biblical characters, and record their answers.

After every group has had a chance to interview two characters, read each question from the handout and allow the group members to give their responses. Next, distribute the Bibles and choose several individuals to read 1 Peter 2:11-12 aloud. Discuss the following questions:

- What do you think these verses mean? (*We're supposed to view life on earth in the same way as those Old Testament characters you interviewed earlier. Our actions should show that we're people of another culture—the culture of heaven!*)

- What does it mean to "live such good lives among the pagans" (*The word "pagan" originally just meant "villager, rustic or civilian," but it came to be associated with those who worshiped local gods. Today it means that we are to live for Jesus among people in our lives who don't know God.*)

- Why would people who don't know God accuse a Christian of "doing wrong"? (*Christians wouldn't be doing what everyone else was doing. When you go against the norms of society, people will react.*)

Choose several individuals to read Galatians 5:16-26. Ask the group members what they think they would have to change or do differently in order to put verses 22-26 into practice in their lives.

Option 2: Aliens on Earth! For this option, you will need several Bibles, copies of "Aliens on Earth!" (found on the next page), pens or pencils and two popular action-figures. (Note: This option has some concepts that are abstract. The group members will grasp the ideas much better by using the handout to write down the points as you discuss them.)

For this option, you will be guiding the group members through a four-step logical approach as to why they should act differently. Distribute "Aliens on Earth!" and pens or pencils. Next, bring out the action figures. Designate one of the figures to represent a person who knows God (such as them) and another action figure to represent a person who does not know God (maybe one of their friends at school). Don't be afraid to really ham it up and use different voices for the figures. Again, this will help students visualize what you're saying.

Aliens on Earth!

As a Christian, you are . . .

_____

_____

_____

_____

_____

_____

_____

That makes you . . .

_____

_____

_____

_____

_____

_____

_____

You should live by the . . .

_____

_____

_____

_____

_____

_____

_____

Which means you will . . .

_____

_____

_____

_____

_____

_____

Next, designate places in the room to represent "heaven" and "earth." This could be a corner of the room, a table, or any other location. When you talk about being a citizen of heaven, take the action figure that represents the Christian to the place that represents heaven (such as the right side of the room). When you talk about being a visitor on earth, bring the Christian figure from heaven over to visit the other figure who is on earth. Here are the answers on the handout that the group members will need to fill in as you talk:

- As a Christian, you are . . . <u>a citizen of heaven</u>.
- That makes you . . . <u>a visitor on earth</u>.
- You should live by . . . <u>the values of heaven</u>.
- Which means you will . . . <u>act differently on earth</u>.

Distribute Bibles and choose two group members to read Hebrews 11:13-16 and 1 Peter 2:11-12 aloud. Discuss the following questions:

- Both passages refer to being "aliens and strangers" on earth. What does this mean? (*In the passage from Hebrews, the author is talking about the heroes of the faith—Noah, Abraham, Sarah and others—who lived for God in a culture that worshiped other gods. This made them stand out in a crowd. In the 1 Peter passage, the author is telling Christians that they will also stand out because of their faith.*)

- According to Peter, why do sinful desires war against our souls? (*We are living in a world in which the enemy has a lot of room to maneuver and tempt us to sin. It is a constant battle every day to resist the influence of the world and live for God.*)

- What is the point in living "good lives" in front of others? (*So others will see our lives and realize something is different about us. When we allow God to use us, we reflect His nature, and this will draw people to Him.*)

- Why would some people accuse those who live "good lives" as being wrongdoers? (*Because the good they are doing is different from what society expects of them. Their concept of "good" could be different from that of God.*)

Choose several individuals to read Galatians 5:16-26. Ask the group what they think they would have to change or do differently in order to put verses 22-26 into practice at school.

DIG

Option 1: Picture This. For this option, you will need a few very old middle-school or high-school yearbooks (for added fun, use your own if you still have them). Ahead of time, scan or copy the pictures in the yearbooks so you can show them to the group. Find pictures that are the most unusual, funny or even bizarre.

Begin by showing the yearbook pictures to the group. Explain that yearbooks are a great way to capture memories of the place where we spend most of our waking hours: school. Next, ask the group members to respond to the following questions:

- How would your life at school be different if you really lived for Christ 100 percent of the time?
- Have you ever had someone tell you that you seem different?
- Was it because of Christ, or just because you were being weird?
- Do you know any one at your school who really lives for God?
- What does this person do that makes it obvious he or she is a Christian?
- How would you treat other students if you were really allowing the Holy Spirit to guide your life at school?
- How would other students treat you if you acted this way?
- What do you think they would write about you in your yearbook?
- How do you feel about being different—about standing out as an alien and a stranger?

For teens, the desire to be normal is so great that being considered different is a real challenge. Make sure you spend enough time on this subject to really let your group members share about any anxiety or fear they may be feeling. Share your own experiences, even as an adult, where you have had to make a decision that made you seem different because of your identity in Christ.

Option 2: Deep and Deeper. For this option, you will just need the following case studies and group members who can relate to them. Note that there are two case studies given for this option. Choose the one that you believe your group members can best relate to right now.

Case Study #1: Deep
Terrance has just finished lunch and is walking down the hall toward his locker. He hears a voice yelling his name, but can't tell where it's coming from. Then he sees Cole, a kid in a couple of his classes, emerge

from the crowd. "Terrance," Cole says, "I've gotta talk to you. What is your deal?"

Terrance, who is a Christian, isn't quite sure what to make of this question. "Huh?" he mumbles. "Did I do something wrong?"

"It's been bugging me for weeks now," Cole explains. "I've been watching you, and you are just flat-out different from everyone else in this school. I mean, I don't want to be rude or anything, but, like, why are you so *different*?"

Discuss the following questions as a group:

• What would you say if you were Terrance?
• How might Cole respond?
• What kinds of things might Cole have seen that would make him think Terrance was different?

Case Study #2: Deeper

Jess was a popular girl—until a few months ago when she made a radical decision to totally live for God. It has been challenging for her to stick with her commitment, and she has been tempted to drop it a bunch of times. Recently, for example, her three best friends told her they didn't want to hang out with her anymore, because she wouldn't gossip or do anything "fun." And Billy Sheridan has started calling her "Jesus freak" all the time. Even the other Christian kids keep their distance from her and say things like, "You're taking this stuff way too seriously, Jess." You don't go to Jess's school, but you are in her youth group. This afternoon, she called and asked you for advice.

Ask the group what advice they would give to Jess in this situation. Would they agree that she is taking her commitment to seriously?

APPLY

Option 1: It's Your Choice. This is a great option if you have people in your group who have not yet made the commitment to follow Christ. As you present the material in this option, you might want to designate one side of your room as "God" and the other as "Humans" to emphasize the gulf between the two. Have Bibles available as gifts for those who make a commitment to Christ.

Begin by explaining that we have been discussing how having a relationship with Jesus makes us different. However, for some in the group, this might not have made much sense, because you haven't yet experienced the most important difference—a relationship with Jesus. God is our Creator and loves us more than we can imagine, but as human beings, we are naturally drawn to do the wrong things. Sin will always pull us to disobey God's Word and do our own thing. This creates a huge chasm that separates us from God.

However, God sent Jesus, His Son, to earth to become a human being just like us and bridge this chasm of sin. Jesus lived a perfectly sinless life on earth for 33 years and then took the punishment for our sins on Himself when He died on the cross. But that's not the end of the story. Jesus came back to life and conquered the sin that had separated us from God. Through His sacrifice, He built a bridge for all people.

State to the group that this leads to a choice that they must make. They can either confess the sin that separates them from God and receive His gift of salvation, or they can ignore Jesus' sacrifice and continue to live under the power of sin. They can ask Jesus to be in charge of their lives and help to help them serve Him every day, or they can try to make the best of their lives totally on their own. Jesus' life, death and resurrection has formed a bridge between them and God. They must choose whether or not they will cross that bridge and accept Jesus as their Savior and Lord.

Invite any group members who would like to ask Jesus to come into their lives to pray the following prayer, repeating after you: "Dear Jesus, I know I'm a sinner. I've missed the mark and I feel empty. I need you, and I turn my life over to you. Help me to obey you every day and be different from those around me." Close by asking those who prayed that prayer for the first time to come forward to receive a gift Bible. Congratulate each person on his or her new life in Jesus! Write down names, phone numbers, home addresses and email addresses of those who made this decision. Contact them in the coming week and encourage them to get involved with a church (yours or someone else's).

Option 2: Letters to Live By. For this option, you will need paper and pens or pencils. If your group members seem ready to "go for it" in regard to sharing their faith, invite them to make their commitment firm by writing a letter to someone to tell him or her about it. The catch? They have to write the letter to someone at their school (this can be a friend, a teacher, the librarian and so on). Let them know that they need to share with this person how they plan on changing so they will be living more like Jesus.

Before the group members write this letter, make sure they understand how important it is for them to follow through on what they write. Give them some time to draft the letter, and let them know that you are available if they have any questions. When the group is finished, close in prayer. Ask Jesus to help the people who will read the letters to be able to see Christ in your students. Ask God to help them live out what they have written in their letters.

REFLECT

The following short devotions are for the group members to reflect on and answer during the week. You can make a copy of these pages and distribute to your class or download and print from **www.gospellight.com/uncommon/jh_dealing_with_pressure.zip**.

1—INSIDE OUT

Check out Exodus 34:29-35. Imagine that you are waiting at the bottom of Mt. Sinai when Moses comes down the mountain. How are you able to tell that Moses has been with God?

- ❐ He is wearing a T-shirt that says, "I've been with God!"
- ❐ He is carrying around two heavy stone tablets.
- ❐ His face appears to be . . . glowing.
- ❐ He's humming a catchy worship tune.

Now think about how others around you might know that you are a Christian. Would they be able to tell because:

- ❐ You're wearing a T-shirt with Bible verses and little fish on it?
- ❐ You're carrying around a 15-pound Bible wherever you go?
- ❐ Your life seems somehow different?
- ❐ You're singing "Jesus Loves Me" in both English and Spanish?

Some of these things may be true if you're a Christian—but your life should definitely look different to those who do not know Jesus. Becoming a Christian makes you a new creation, which begins on the *inside*, but as you spend more and more time getting to know God, changes will take place on the *outside* as well. You might not end up glowing like Moses did, but the changes that God makes in you will stand out just as brightly to everyone around you.

2—THE EXTRA MILE

Flip open that there Bible to Luke 6:27-31.

Maria really bugs you. Every day she asks to borrow money for lunch, and she never even thanks you for lending it to her—or pays you back. She "forgets" to do her science homework, and then every Thursday she asks to copy yours. At least once a week she borrows a pen, but she never gives it back.

Now Maria has really gone too far. She is telling people that you said some mean things about Kim, but all you ever said was that you were too tired to go over to Kim's house after school. What you really want to do is yell at Maria! You're tempted to tell everyone what a leech she is. It would serve her right!

But wait a minute. What did that verse in Luke say? Did Jesus really ask you to love people who are your enemies—which includes people who hurt you or say mean things about you? This doesn't mean that you let people abuse you, but you need to do the right thing with a loving attitude. In your case, this might mean putting a little distance between yourself and Maria and not letting her borrow your stuff all the time.

Is there anybody who is bugging you? Do you find yourself wanting to get even with this person? Do you want to annoy or hurt them back? If so, read this Scripture passage again and ask Jesus how you can go the extra mile with the person who is bugging you. Spend a few minutes praying for that person today, asking God to give you compassion for him or her.

3—GOOD NEWS/BAD NEWS

Use those sharp eyes of yours to read John 9:13-34.

If you knew a way that everybody could get a million dollars (yourself included), how would you spread the news?

- ❏ Get your own webpage with some cool links to other sites.
- ❏ Rent a blimp and drop birds from it that have messages strapped around their necks.
- ❏ Learn how to fly a plane and tie a sign behind it with information on how to get the money.
- ❏ Dress up like a dollar bill and stand on a corner.

It's amazing how when you have good news you want to share it. That's how the blind man whom Jesus healed in John 9:13-34 felt. The man couldn't wait to share it with his neighbors.

You have the best news ever—that Jesus offers new life and new hope to everybody. He has changed you from the inside out, and He is ready and waiting to help others make changes as well. Spend two minutes praying for two people that you know who haven't yet let Jesus make a difference in their lives.

4—BETTER THAN EVER

Race to 1 Corinthians 4:6-7. I mean it—now—run!

Betty the Baptist hardly ever talks to Paul the Presbyterian. Sometimes Cathy the Catholic tries to talk to Betty, Paul or even Ethan the Episcopalian and Martin the Methodist, but all they ever talk about is how cool their own youth groups and youth pastors are.

Thinking your kind of Christianity is better than what others have is a kind of pride. The Bible tells us that we are not to have pride in anything except for what Jesus has done for us. Although Christians are different from those who don't follow Jesus, we do have much in common with other Christians. We have all received the gifts of salvation and forgiveness. Note that these things are *gifts* and not *rewards* we have somehow earned. It's not our youth pastors or our churches or even our youth groups that make us different. It is Jesus!

Is pride an issue in your life? If so, what can you do about it?

_____

_____

_____

Think about some of the kids at your school who don't go to church. What type of things could you do that would make them see you are different?

_____

_____

_____

What are some practical ways you can show God's love to others today?

_____

_____

_____

Ask God to give you the opportunity and the words to tell others about Jesus. He will do it!

THE PRESSURE OF LIVING WITH INTEGRITY

THE BIG IDEA

Following Christ requires a life of integrity in every situation.

SESSION AIMS

In this session, you will guide group members to (1) learn what integrity is; (2) think about how they handle the pressure of temptation—especially at school; and (3) create a plan that will help them to maintain their integrity this week.

THE BIGGEST VERSE

"Don't let anyone look down on you because you are young, but set an example for the believers in speech, in conduct, in love, in faith and in purity" (1 Timothy 4:12).

OTHER IMPORTANT VERSES

Psalm 25:21; Proverbs 10:9; 11:3; 12:3; 19:1; Matthew 22:15-22; Mark 11:15-18; 12:13-17; Luke 16:13; 2 Corinthians 9:7; 1 John 1:8

Note: Additional options and worksheets in 8^1/$_2$" x 11" format for this session are available for download at **www.gospellight.com/uncommon/jh_dealing_with_pressure.zip**.

STARTER

Option 1: Move It. For this option, you will need several sturdy chairs. Ahead of time, arrange the chairs in rows as you might find in a classroom. Make sure that you leave space between the chairs so the group members will be able to move to the chair in front of them or in back of them.

Welcome the students and ask them what they think the word "temptation" means. (*To entice to do wrong by the promise of pleasure or gain.*) Now ask them what the word "integrity" means. (*When something or someone is what it is—nothing is hidden or fake.*) Explain that today, the group will be discussing these two concepts, and you will begin by playing a short game.

State to the group that you are going to read a list of statements, along with a direction of movement and the number of seats to move. If this statement is *false* for the group member, he or she needs to stay in his or her seat. If it is true for the group member, however, he or she needs to move the number and direction of seats indicated. If another person is in that seat already, the person who is moving to that seat must cram into that seat beside him or her. If two are already on that seat, the person who is moving must sit on the next chair. If a group member reaches the end of the row of chairs, he or she must circle back to the other end.

After explaining the instructions, make sure everyone is sitting down. Go over a few ground rules, such as no fighting over chairs, to make sure that no one gets hurt. Begin the game by reading the following list, pausing after each statement so the group members can move.

- If you've ever . . . lied about something, move one seat to the right.
- If you've ever . . . cheated on a test or quiz, move two seats to the left.
- If you've ever . . . been nice to someone only so he or she would be nice to you, move one seat forward.
- If you've ever . . . made up a fake excuse about homework you didn't do, move three seats to the right.
- If you've ever . . . copied the answers to homework from someone else, move two seats backward.
- If you've ever . . . asked to be excused to go to the restroom when you didn't actually have to go, move four seats to the left.
- If you've ever . . . taken something from someone else's lunch when they weren't looking, move one seat forward.
- If you've ever . . . pretended to know what you were doing when you didn't, move two seats to the right.

- If you've ever . . . lied to your parents, move three seats backward.
- If you've ever . . . pretended to be sick so you didn't have to go to school, move five seats to the left.
- If you've ever . . . pretended to be hurt so you didn't have to participate in gym class, move two seats to the right.
- If you've ever . . . lacked integrity, go back to your original seat.

Wrap up by explaining that we all give in to temptation and sin at times, but as followers of Jesus Christ, God wants us to live lives of integrity.

Option 2: I Said It, I'll Do It. For this option, you will need one copy of "I Said It, I'll Do It" (found on the following page), a prize that the winning team can share, and a hat, a box or a bag. Ahead of time, cut the handout into individual slips and place the slips into the hat. (Note: If your group is typically large or if you plan to play several rounds of the game, cut three or four copies of the handout into strips and place all of them into the hat.)

Welcome the group members and divide them into at least three teams. Ask each team to choose one person to be its representative, and then have all the representatives come forward. One at a time, each representative will select a slip from the hat and read the action listed. When everyone has selected a slip with one action, ask all of the representatives to perform their actions. Once this is complete, have the representatives tell the rest of the group what the action was supposed to be.

Award 100 points to those who perform their tasks to your satisfaction. Play as many rounds as you want, and award a prize to the team with the most points at the end of the rounds. The point of this game is to show the group members that they really need to do what they have said they will do—which is a key component of integrity. After all, it's easy to talk the talk, but it's not always easy to walk the talk! When the game is over, discuss the following questions:

- What is integrity? (*When something or someone is what it is—nothing is hidden or fake.*)
- How does having integrity affect the way that you are able to be an example for others? (*If you have integrity, you will automatically be an example to other people.*)
- How does having integrity help you to resist the pressure of temptation? (*If you have integrity, you will be able to recognize temptation for what it is and, with God's help, not be deceived by it.*)

I SAID IT
I'LL DO IT

I will run up to someone and give that person a bear hug.

I will sing the national anthem.

I will perform a disco dance.

I will act like I'm dying.

I will be a tiger—a big, mean one!

I will recite a poem of my own creation.

I will run around like a chicken.

I will impersonate my youth leader.

I will pretend to play in a championship Ping-Pong match with an imaginary friend.

I will rub my stomach and pat my head at the same time.

I will impersonate a popular singer.

I will impersonate an auctioneer.

I will tickle someone.

I will be a chimpanzee showing off in a zoo.

- How does doing what you say you will do affect your integrity? (*It shows others that you can be trusted to tell and to be the truth.*)

MESSAGE

Option 1: Multiple-choice Melodramas. For this option, you will need several Bibles and a copy of "Multiple-choice Melodramas" (found on the next page).

Recruit four volunteers to act in a set of three dramas. (Be sure to select group members who are willing to play the parts and do the actions). One volunteer will play the part of Jesus, while the other three volunteers will play the parts of the Pharisees. The group members in the audience will be "the crowd." Instruct the Pharisees to sit together in the middle of the crowd.

Explain to the volunteers that all three dramas they will be acting out are based on the same Bible story. The volunteers will need to act out their parts as you, the leader, read them aloud. If a volunteer's character speaks in the drama, that person should repeat it after you read it.

When all the dramas are finished, pass out the Bibles. Ask the group members to look up Mark 12:13-17, and then read the passage.[1] Have the group members vote for the drama that was closest to the real Bible story. (The answer would be the third drama.) After this, discuss the following questions:

- Why did the Pharisees begin by stating they knew Jesus was a man of integrity? (*They were attempting to flatter Him because they wanted to trap Him and prove that He didn't have integrity.*)

- Did their plan work? (*No, what happened was just the opposite of what they wanted. Jesus didn't listen to their flattery. He spoke the truth regardless of how it would affect Him, and in doing so proved that He was a man of integrity.*)

- Why did the Pharisees ask Him the question about taxes? (*The Romans required the Jews to pay tribute money into the emperor's treasury. Some Jews, like the Zealots, refused to pay; some, like the Pharisees, disliked paying, but usually did it anyway; and some, like the Herodians, had no objection to paying. The question was intended to trap Jesus. In their view, He only had two options in answering: the people should pay taxes or that they shouldn't. If Jesus said the people should pay taxes, He would offend many Jews by going against His own teachings, which said everything belonged to God. If He said the people shouldn't pay taxes, He would place*)

MULTIPLE-CHOICE MELODRAMAS

(Based on Mark 12:13-17)

VERSION ONE

Jesus was teaching a group of people something important. The people were listening, nodding and making noises of agreement. Then three Pharisees raised their hands and asked together, "Hey, Jesus, what is integrity?" The crowd stood silent, their mouths hanging open, waiting for Jesus' response. Jesus answered, "Integrity is being the same person on the inside as you are on the outside." The crowd knew that the Pharisees did not have integrity, so they pointed at them and laughed loudly while shouting, "No integrity! No integrity!"

VERSION TWO

Jesus was teaching a group of people something important. The people were listening, nodding and making noises of agreement. Then three Pharisees stood up in the middle of the crowd and yelled, "Hey, Jesus!" The crowd was visibly shocked. They started yelling at the Pharisees, "Sit down!" and "Be quiet!" Jesus silenced the crowd and then turned to the Pharisees. "Do you have a question?" He asked. They said, in perfect unison, "Who is Caesar?" The crowd groaned. Jesus answered, "He's the guy who has his face stamped on our coins." The crowd roared with laughter and approval, and then a few of them chased the Pharisees away.

VERSION THREE

Jesus was teaching a group of people something important. The people were listening, nodding and making noises of agreement. Then three Pharisees stood up and said, "Jesus, we know You are a man of integrity." The crowd became quiet, waiting with eagerness to see what would happen next. A couple of them were so eager they fell off their chairs! The Pharisees took out some coins and asked, "Is it right to pay taxes to Caesar?" Now the crowd was even more eager, because they knew that any answer Jesus gave could get Him in trouble. A few more members of the crowd fell off their chairs with eagerness. Jesus looked at their coins and calmly asked, "Whose picture is on this coin?" The Pharisees answered, "Caesar's." Jesus continued, "Give to Caesar what is Caesar's and to God what is God's." The Pharisees knew they hadn't trapped Jesus, and they left the room muttering and sputtering and whining. The crowd, amazed at Jesus' wisdom, gasped in perfect unison.

Himself in a dangerous position against the Roman government by dis-obeying Roman law. Either way, He would be doing the wrong thing, which would prove He didn't have integrity.)

- How did Jesus' answer show He had integrity? (*He answered the Phar-isees in a way they didn't expect. He told them to give back what belonged to Caesar to Caesar and what belonged to God to God. The meaning be-hind His answer was: Pay your taxes as you should to Caesar, but remem-ber that everything you have belongs to God. Jesus' whole life showed that He lived up to this standard. He took care of his responsibilities to others, but He always put God first in everything.*)

Next, read Proverbs 10:9 to the group. Discuss the following questions:

- What does it mean to have a secure walk with God? (*It means you are living the way God wants you to live and He is pleased with you.*)

- How did Jesus' actions and words make His walk secure? (*Jesus lived the way God wanted Him to live, so God was always pleased with Him.*)

Close by reading 1 Timothy 4:12 and discussing the following questions:

- In what ways do you think this verse is a big part of what integrity is? (*It tells us to be a right example of what God wants through our speech, conduct, love, faith and purity—things that please God.*)

- Do you think that only older people can have integrity? (*No, people of any age can choose to live with or without integrity. But the earlier you make it a practice, the better it is for you and your Christian witness.*)

- Paul mentions "speech," "conduct," "love," "faith" and "purity." Is there anything else that he left out? (*Allow students to respond.*)

Conclude by stating that Jesus gave us a model of integrity to follow. When-ever we are struggling with maintaining our integrity, we can turn to the Bible and see what Christ did in different situations. We can also turn to Him and ask for His help.

Option 2: Real or Plastic? For this option, you will need several Bibles, a piece of plastic fruit, and a real piece of the same kind of fruit.

Begin by explaining that "integrity" means being what we say we are and following through with what we say we will do. Hold up the plastic piece of fruit and tell the group that you are holding an orange (or apple, banana, or whatever you chose) in this hand. Now hold up the real piece of fruit and tell the group that you are also holding an orange in your other hand. Ask them what they think the difference is between the two. (The answer would be that one is *really* an orange and one is just *pretending* to be an orange.)

Explain that the same thing is true of people. Some people say they are honest, but when you get down to it they really are not. Some people make a commitment to do something or to be somewhere, but they don't follow through. Some people say they are followers of Christ, but don't really live like Jesus at all.

Continue by stating that Jesus showed integrity all the time. One example is found in Matthew 22:15-22. Read the passage aloud, and then ask the following questions:

- Why did the Pharisees begin by stating they knew Jesus was a man of integrity and that he taught "the way of God in accordance with the truth"? (*They were attempting to flatter Him because they wanted to trap Him and to prove that He didn't have integrity.*)

- Why did they think asking a question about paying *taxes* would set a good trap for Him? (*Back in Jesus' time, like today, the government required its citizens to pay taxes to the state. In this case, the Jews were required to pay taxes to the Romans, a foreign power that had taken control in the region. Different groups of Jews had different reactions to this. Some, such as the Herodians, had ties to the Romans and had no problem paying. Others, such as the Zealots, rejected all things Roman and refused to pay. Still others, such as the Pharisees themselves, didn't like paying taxes but went along with it. In asking the question, the Pharisees were trying to force Jesus into saying that people should pay taxes or they shouldn't. If Jesus told the people they should pay taxes to Caesar, he would offend someone from one of these groups. If He said they shouldn't, the Romans would see Him as a troublemaker. Either way, He would be doing the wrong thing, which would prove He didn't have integrity.*)

- Did the plan work? (*No. Jesus didn't listen to their flattery. He spoke the truth regardless of how it would affect Him and in doing this proved He was a man of integrity.*)

- How did Jesus' answer show that He had integrity? (*Jesus had a coin brought to Him and asked whose portrait and inscription was on it. When the people answered "Caesar," He told them to give what belonged to Caesar to Caesar, and what belonged to God to God. In other words, they should pay their taxes to Caesar, but remember that everything they have and are belongs to God. Jesus' whole life showed that He lived up to this standard. He took care of His responsibilities to others, but He always put God first in everything.*)

Conclude by stating that integrity isn't proven by what we say but by what we do. The *saying* part only sets us up to prove whether or not we have integrity—it's in the *doing* that the proof is shown. Hold up the plastic fruit again and explain that a person might not realize this isn't an orange until he or she holds it and tries to bite into it. The same is true for us. Others will recognize that we are the real thing by what we do. When we follow Christ's example and always seek to do those things that are pleasing to God, others will recognize us by our fruit and be drawn to Him.

DIG

Option 1: We Have a Situation. For this option, you will need copies of "We Have a Situation" (found on the next page). Begin by dividing the students into groups of four to five people, and then give each group a different situation from the handout. Have them answer the questions listed at the bottom of the sheet. When they are finished, read the questions out loud and allow each group to give its answers. Here are the questions:

- What would this person need to do in order to have integrity?
- What might be the consequences in this situation if he or she doesn't have integrity?
- What might be the consequences if he or she *does* have integrity?

Conclude by stating that every action we take in life will result in one consequence or another. If we choose to do what God says, even if it is difficult, and make a stand for what we believe, then our faith will grow and others will see us as having integrity. On the other hand, if we choose to do what the world says, our relationship with God will be affected, and others will see us as lacking integrity.

We Have a Situation

Situation One

Megan really wants to be accepted. She feels she can only fit in if she flirts with boys and acts dumb, because all the popular girls at school act that way.

Situation Two

Mike has to do a history project with Sam. Sam is super smart and very willing to do all the work. Mike has agreed to research a certain part of their project, but he knows that if he doesn't do it, Sam will do it without complaining.

Situation Three

Sarah's friend Jessie knows an answer on the test that Sarah can't remember. Jessie has her paper where Sarah can see it, and Sarah knows that her friend wouldn't mind if she peeked. The teacher is helping another student at the front of the room, so there is no danger of being caught.

Situation Four

Phil did a stupid thing. He accidentally started a rumor about his friend Zack. Later, Zack asks him if he started the rumor. Phil knows that if he denies starting it, Zack will believe him.

Discussion Questions

1. What would this person need to do in order to have integrity?
2. What might be the consequences in this situation if he or she doesn't have integrity?
3. What might be the consequences in this situation if he or she does have integrity?

Option 2: Just a Little Cheating. For this option, you will need just the following story about good ol' Jerod and the questions that follow. Begin by reading this case study to the group:

> Jerod is frustrated. He wants to live totally for Jesus, but he knows that means he has to act like Jesus would want him to act at school. For him, that means no cheating, even though all the other kids do it—including the Christians. It's so easy. His teachers never catch him, and no one's bugging him about it—except Jesus! And it's not like anyone has ever come up to him and said, "Jerod, I can't believe in Jesus because you don't have integrity." Jerod is having a tough time figuring out why cheating on a test or two is such a big deal.

Discuss the following questions:

- What would you say to Jerod?
- So what if he cheats a little bit? Who is it going to hurt?
- What if he decides not to cheat quite so often? Is that good enough?

Conclude by stating that in life, we are faced with difficult choices like these each day. Oftentimes, what we feel God is asking us to do seems insignificant in the moment, but the truth is that our actions always have long-term consequences that we may not be able to see at the present time. In these situations, we have to trust that God knows what is best and that He is asking us to follow His commands for a reason. It is not always easy, but it is always the right thing to do, and we will build integrity as a result.

APPLY

Option 1: Integrity Plan. For this option, you will need your Bible, index cards and pens or pencils. Begin by stating that we all lack integrity from time to time. However, one way we can build our integrity is to figure out the areas in which we are having problems and change those areas.

Read 1 John 1:9 to the group. State that a great way to get back on track when we are struggling in this area is to confess our lack of integrity to Jesus. As this passage states, when we confess our sins, Jesus forgives us and cleanses us. This gets us back on track. With Jesus' power, we can change our ways so that we will act with integrity.

Distribute the index cards. Ask the group members to write down one time during the past two weeks when they have shown a lack of integrity and haven't been a good example to those around them. (Note that it will be easier for your group members to be open and honest about their struggles if you volunteer an example from your own life first.)

Ask the group members to turn over their cards and write a plan of action for how they will show integrity in the future when a similar situation arises. State that this will require courage on their part to follow through, but that they will reap the benefits when they choose to live with integrity. Close in prayer, asking God to guide each student through his or her plan of action.

Option 2: Integrity Roleplay. For this option, you will only need your group members.

Explain to the group that a person's degree of integrity speaks loudly about his or her relationship with Jesus—and, believe it or not, others are listening! Choose two volunteers to come forward, and then read the following scenario:

> You are a Christian, and one day you are caught in a lie that you told. Last Friday, you were invited by your friend John to attend the school football game, but you said you had to do homework. Actually, you thought you might have the chance to attend a professional baseball game with another group of friends, but you didn't want to hurt John's feelings because he wasn't invited, so you lied. Now John has found out about it, and he is angry. He confronts you about your lie in front of Juanita, a non-Christian friend to whom you've been trying to witness all year. During lunch, Juanita asks why you lied, especially since you're supposed to be a Christian.

Assign the role of the Christian to one of the volunteers and the role of Juanita to the other. Let them know that they're going to continue the story by

Youth Leader Tip

Your students can get tired of hearing you talk. Switch it up by having students and adult volunteers share, read Scripture, pray, role-play and even teach the group.

talking to each other in character. If an audience member wants to participate at any point, he or she should yell "freeze!" The actors will then stop talking and freeze in position. The person who yelled "freeze" will take the place of the character he or she chooses and resume the dialogue. Allow the group members to continue this exercise for 5 to 10 minutes.

When the roleplay is over, explain to the group that while it might sound strange, whenever people realize that we aren't perfect just because we're Christians, it actually gives us chances to share about Jesus with them. After all, if we *were* perfect, we wouldn't need Jesus. We need Jesus not only for our salvation but also to help us in our everyday lives. He can give us the strength and the desire to do the right thing.

Invite the group members to pray silently for someone in their lives who needs Jesus. Give them a minute or two to do this, and then close with a prayer asking Jesus to help the students use their relationship with Him in a way that will attract others.

REFLECT

The following short devotions are for the group members to reflect on and answer during the week. You can make a copy of these pages and distribute to your class or download and print from **www.gospellight.com/uncommon/jh_dealing_with_pressure.zip.**

1—TO TELL THE TRUTH

What's wrong with a little lie? Turn to Proverbs 12:3 to find out.

Lynda hated it when her mom made her go over to Shauna's house. The only reason she had to go was because her mom was friends with Shauna's mom. Lynda thought Shauna was totally boring, and there was nothing fun to do at her house. Shauna's family didn't have cable TV and only kept health food around the house.

On Thursday afternoon, Shauna called and asked Lynda if she wanted to come over for a few hours. Lynda didn't want to go, so she lied and said she didn't feel well. Lynda's mom was in the room and heard her say this.

About 20 minutes later, Lynda got a phone call from Carl, a guy from church whom she liked. He invited Lynda to go skateboarding with him. Lynda raced downstairs to ask her mom if she could go. Her mom said, "I'm sorry, honey, but not this time. After all, you said you weren't feeling well, so you need to stay home."

If you were Lynda, what should you have done in this situation?

_____

_____

_____

What does Proverbs 12:3 say about the importance of having integrity?

_____

_____

_____

One lie always leads to another, because when you lie, you have to *keep* adding lies to cover your tracks. Over time, people will not believe you when you *are* telling the truth. *So, it's always better to tell the truth in the first place, even if it is inconvenient.* This week, ask God to help you always tell the truth, even if your first thought is to tell a lie.

2—CHOOSE THE BEST

If you care about what people think about you, read Proverbs 19:1.

Imagine for a moment that you are a cab driver and you took some passengers home after a concert. When you get to their house, you tell them that their cab fare is $15. However, they will only pay $10. No matter what you say, they refuse to pay more, so you decide to let it go.

The next day, you find one of the passenger's wallets. Inside there are four $5 bills, along with a telephone number. What would you do?

- ☐ Take all four of the $5 bills and deposit the wallet in the nearest trash can. After all, they deserve it for not paying you.
- ☐ Take just the $5 you are owed and give the rest to a needy person.
- ☐ Take just the $5 and then give the owner of the wallet a call.
- ☐ Call the person first without taking any money.

In fact, this situation actually happened, and the cab driver chose to give the person a call without taking any money. When the passenger realized how honest the cab driver was, she paid him what she owed him, and give him a tip as well.

Today, you're probably going to have some choices to make about how you will act in certain situations. Ask God to show you how to do the right thing, even if it won't necessarily be easy.

3—INTEGRITY IS THE GOAL

If you'd like to do what is right, check out Psalm 25:21.

All the kids in Natalie's group were going out to smash mailboxes on Halloween. Natalie wanted to hang out with her friends. She was tempted to go with them, but she knew deep inside that it wouldn't be the right thing to do, so she didn't go.

The day after Halloween, Natalie called her friend Paige to see how it went. Paige's mom answered the phone, and she wouldn't let Natalie talk to Paige. "Is something wrong?" Natalie asked. Paige's mom answered, "You should be glad you weren't with Paige and her friends last night. They were arrested for vandalism when they were caught destroying people's mailboxes. Paige won't be talking to anyone on the phone—or going out with her friends for that matter—for a long time."

In this story, the direct consequence was that Paige got arrested. What are some of the other consequences that she will have to face in the future?

_____

_____

_____

_____

Why was it hard for Natalie to decide to *not* go along with the group? Why was this ultimately the best choice?

_____

_____

_____

_____

Doing the right thing protects us from all sorts of bad stuff. Sure, you might not get to do everything your friends are doing, but you won't get in trouble, and you'll know deep down inside that you're making the right decisions. You will have integrity.

Today, ask God to help you make the right choices today. Who knows? Your friends might even follow your choices!

4—MAKING MONEY STRETCH

What's the problem with *really* loving money? Read Haggai 1:5-6 to find one reason.

Long ago, the Temple of God was old and in need of repair. The people told each other they didn't need to rebuild God's house, because they didn't want to give up what they had to help rebuild it. This was a major problem, because the people were supposed to be looking to God for all their needs.

So the Lord spoke to the people through the prophet Haggai. God said they were living in nice houses with paneled walls while His house was a wreck. Then God told them something we should all remember. He said, "You've spent a lot of money, but you haven't got much to show for it. You keep eating and drinking, but you're always hungry and thirsty. You put on layer after layer of clothes, but you can't get warm. You earn money, but you never keep it."

The way you handle your money has a lot to do with your integrity. If you let money or things control you, like the people in the story did, you'll have a hard time understanding that God is in control.

Do you give some of the money you earn to your church? Why or why not?

_____

_____

_____

Based on this passage, what do you think God is asking you to do?

_____

_____

_____

Any money you get comes from God, and He asks you to give just a little of it back to Him (this is called a tithe). So today, if you are having trouble living with integrity in the area of your money, pray and ask God to help you. For as Paul wrote, "God loves a cheerful giver" (2 Corinthians 9:7)!

THE PRESSURE TO GOSSIP

THE BIG IDEA
Everything you say about others should help them and not hurt them.

SESSION AIMS
In this session, you will guide group members to (1) learn what gossip is; (2) understand what it feels like to have someone gossip about them; and (3) make a commitment to God to stop gossiping.

THE BIGGEST VERSE
"Those who consider themselves religious and yet do not keep a tight rein on their tongues deceive themselves, and their religion is worthless" (James 1:26).

OTHER IMPORTANT VERSES
Proverbs 10:19; 11:13; 16:28; 18:8,13,21; 20:19; 26:20; 2 Corinthians 12:20; Ephesians 4:29; James 1:19; 3:1-12

Note: Additional options and worksheets in 8¹/₂" x 11" format for this session are available for download at **www.gospellight.com/uncommon/jh_dealing_with_pressure.zip**.

STARTER

Option 1: Rumor Slips. For this option, you will need "Rumor Slips" (found on the next page), a picture of an anonymous young teen, and a way to show the picture to the whole group. The teen could have a nametag with "Hello, my name is Chris" written on it. Copy and cut "Rumor Slips" into individual slips of paper and fold them in half. (Note that if you have fewer than 11 students, this game will be difficult to play.)

Begin by greeting the group members and distributing the rumor slips. As you do, inform them that they are each being given a rumor about a make-believe teen named Chris. Stress to the group that they must keep the information they receive about Chris to themselves until the game begins.

When you give the signal, the students will need to get into groups of two people each and ask each other, "What have you heard about Chris?" Next, each partner will whisper the rumor that he or she has on his or her rumor slip. When you give the signal again, students must switch partners. The new partners will need to whisper their own rumors and the ones they were just told.

Repeat the process four times, and then have everyone return to his or her seat. Read the rumors on the slips aloud one at a time. If any of the group members heard the rumor that is being read, they should raise their hands and say, "I heard that!" The point of this game is to see which rumors will spread the most.

Transition by explaining that life is often like this. Rumors get spread, and people like Chris get hurt. Today, the group members will be learning what the Bible has to say about rumors and gossip and how to make a difference in the way they act around their friends and at school

Option 2: Down the Line. For this option, you will need paper, pens or pencils and a prize for the winning team. Ahead of time, write down a sentence that could be easily mixed up by the time it is passed from person to person. If you can't come up with one, here is a suggestion: "The frog jumped on the top of the metal roof at 12:00, counted 11 stars and 9 planets, skipped to the aluminum chimney, and slid down the bronze rain gutter."

Begin by welcoming the group members and selecting an impartial judge for the game. Divide the group into teams of 10 students each. (If your group is smaller, just have one team, but make it noncompetitive.)

Have the teams form two lines and distribute a piece of paper and a pen or pencil to the person at the end of each line. Explain that the teams will be participating in a gossip competition. You will be whispering a sentence into the ear of the first person, that person will turn and whisper the message into

RUMOR SLIPS

RUMOR 1
I heard that the new kid is really weird. He's missing his left big toe.

RUMOR 2
Hey, do you know that new guy? I heard he's served time in prison.

RUMOR 3
You won't believe what I heard about the new boy in class. He flunked the fourth grade—twice!

RUMOR 4
I heard something interesting about the new kid. He used to be super rich!

RUMOR 5
You know that new guy in our school? He had to leave his last school because he burned it down.

the next person's ear, and so on down the line. The last person to hear the sentence will write it exactly as he or she heard it on the piece of paper provided. The person should *not* let anyone else see it.

As the game progresses, the impartial judge needs to keep track of how much time it takes each team to pass the message to the end of the line and write it down. The team that completes the task in the shortest amount of time will receive 100 points, the second fastest team will receive 75 points, and so on, reducing the points by 25 for each subsequent place. After you read the original sentence aloud, the students at the end of each line will read what they have written on their papers. The impartial judge will award from 0 to 75 points to each team depending on how accurate the message was.

Total the points and award prizes to the winning team. Explain that this same thing often happens in our lives. A rumor starts, and by the end of the day, it has been totally blown out of proportion. Today, the group members are going to learn how to act radically different when they hear rumors and gossip.

MESSAGE

Option 1: Which Is Correct? For this option, you need several Bibles. Begin by reading the following verse pairings from Proverbs. For each pair, the verse with an asterisk represents the real verse, while the other verse is . . . well, slightly modified. Don't tell students which one is the correct verse as you read them.

Proverbs 11:13
1. A gossip betrays a confidence, but a trustworthy person keeps a secret.*
2. Gossip is everywhere, so be careful what secrets you share.

Proverbs 16:28
1. Gossip can destroy friendships, but it's something you can't avoid.
2. A perverse person stirs up conflict, and a gossip separates close friends.*

Proverbs 18:8
1. The words of a gossip are like choice morsels; they go down to the inmost parts.*
2. The words of a gossip go in one ear and out the other; it doesn't really affect you.

Proverbs 20:19
1. A gossip betrays a confidence, but may not gossip about you.
2. A gossip betrays a confidence; so avoid anyone who talks too much.*

Proverbs 26:20
1. Without wood a fire goes out; without a gossip a quarrel dies down.*
2. He who gossips about another wins the fight.

After you read each verse in the pair, ask the group members to indicate which they think is the real one. Reveal the correct answer and then read the next pairing. Once you are finished, distribute Bibles and point out that the issue of gossip is not only discussed in the book of Proverbs. In fact, Paul spoke about gossip in 2 Corinthians 12:20 and James spoke about it in James 1:26. Read these verses aloud, and then discuss the following questions as the group:

- What does it mean to keep a "tight rein" on your tongue? (*It means that you are careful about what you say. You don't just say anything that comes to mind but give it some thought first.*)
- How does James link the tongue with religion? (*If you aren't careful about what you say—bad-mouthing others, saying the first thing that comes into your mind, and so on—your religion [or what you say you believe] is worthless.*)
- Do you think this is true? (*Allow students to respond.*)
- Does that mean that if you spread gossip and rumors you're not a Christian? (*What makes a person a Christian is receiving Jesus as his or her Savior and Lord. The "religion" that James refers to in 1:26 is the outward acts that you do that are seen by others. In other words, gossip can destroy your credibility as a Christian witness to others.*)

Conclude by stating that the Bible is very specific about how we should avoid getting caught up in gossip. Gossip will not only hurt the other person, but it also hurts us in the process. In addition, as we discussed previously, it will affect our integrity.

Option 2: Talker and Guesser. For this option, you will need several Bibles, a timekeeping device that has a seconds indicator, prizes, a large sheet of paper, and a pen or pencil. Ahead of time, write the following words on the paper: "discord," "jealousy," "fits of rage," "selfish ambition," "slander," "gossip," "arrogance" and "disorder."

Choose four volunteers and break them into two teams. Send one team out of the room (note that you might want to send an adult leader with them to make sure no one wanders down to the corner donut shop). Give one person on the remaining team the paper with the list and instruct him or her to keep it a secret. This person will be the "Talker," while his or her teammate will be the "Guesser." The Talker will describe the words, one at a time, to the Guesser while you (or another adult) keep track of how long it takes the Guesser to get all five words correct.

When the first team is finished, bring in the other team. Once again, designate one teammate to be the Talker and the other to be the Guesser. Repeat the whole process and keep track of the time it takes for the Guesser to get all five words correct. When this team is finished, award the prize to the team that guessed the words in the shortest amount of time.

After the game is over, distribute Bibles to each person in the group. Explain that Paul used all five of these words in one powerful sentence. Select a volunteer to read 2 Corinthians 12:20 aloud, and then discuss the following questions as a group:

- What is discord? (*Verbal fighting or arguing.*)
- What is jealousy? (*Hostility toward a rival or other person who may have an advantage.*)
- What's the difference between anger and fits of rage? (*Anger is the feeling you have when someone hurts you or disappoints you. Fits of rage are destructive ways of displaying anger, such as breaking things or hitting people.*)
- What is "selfish ambition"? (*It's when someone exists only to serve his or her own interests. This person usually thinks he or she is better than others.*)
- What is slander? (*Saying something about a person that is not true and that damages his or her reputation.*)
- What is gossip? (*Sharing information about someone or even a group of people when the information doesn't need to be shared.*)
- What is arrogance? (*Being stuck-up or convinced you're better than others.*)
- What is disorder—and why would it be included in this list? (*The group members will probably know what disorder is, but it's doubtful they will know why it's in this verse. Paul is referring to a problem in the Corinthian church in which people would shout and create disorder during the worship services.*)

Explain that in this passage, Paul listed several serious sins that were going on in the Corinthian church. Ask the group members why they think Paul considered gossip to be as serious as the other things listed. The answer is that when we gossip, we (1) don't treat people with the respect that God's creation deserves, (2) usually say things that are filled with inaccuracies and lies, (3) build ourselves up at the expense of tearing someone else down, and (4) destroy our relationships with others.

Read James 1:26 and discuss the following questions with the group:

- What does it mean to keep a "tight rein" on your tongue? (*Well, when you keep a tight rein on a horse, it means that you keep it under control. The same is true here—you are careful about what you say.*)
- How does James link the tongue and religion? (*People may think they are doing right in God's sight, but if they can't control their words, they are fooling themselves. As Christians, we need to back up what we say with actions.*)
- How have you found this to be true in your life? (*Allow the group members to respond.*)
- Is James saying that if we have a hard time controlling our tongue, we are not really Christians? (*No, the Bible clearly states that what makes a person a Christian is receiving Jesus as his or her Savior and Lord. The "religion" that James is speaking about is the outward acts we do that others see. Gossip can destroy our credibility as a witness to others.*)

Conclude by stating that both James and Paul were very specific in how they stressed the importance of avoiding gossip. As Christians, we need to be showing love to others, but gossip does just the opposite—it tears others down. This is why it is so important not to get caught up in gossip, even when those around us are doing it.

DIG

Option 1: Rachel's Dilemma. For this option, you will need just this case study and some chatty students. Begin by reading the following to the group:

Rachel and her friends gossip all the time, even though she knows it is wrong. She has decided to make a real effort to stop gossiping so much, even though she knows it might make her a bit of an outsider to the group. She was able to convince one friend, April, to try an experiment and hang out for a whole day without gossiping. Unfortunately, they forgot most of the time, and gossiped like crazy. When they did remember the experiment and didn't gossip, they felt as if they didn't have anything to talk about and they got bored. Rachel's mom gossips all the time as well.

Discuss the following questions as a group. Note that some suggested answers have been provided in case the group members get stuck, but try to use the questions to stimulate discussion and don't let them off easy—encourage them to answer honestly and defend their answers.

- What options does Rachel have? (*Rachel's options might be to give up trying, change her friends, pray every day for strength to avoid gossip, and/or develop a support group to help one another not gossip.*)

- What will help Rachel break this pattern? (*She needs to replace gossiping with a more positive action or walk away when gossip begins.*)

- How do you think her friends would respond if she completely stopped gossiping? (*She would get mixed reactions. Some friends might actually start talking about her. But that's a chance she should be willing to take if she knows she's doing the right thing in the eyes of God.*)

- Should she say anything to her mom? (*Yes. Rachel knows gossiping is wrong, so she should share how she feels about it. Who knows? Her mom might join her in her resolve to stop gossiping.*)

Conclude by asking the group to think of some times during the previous week when they might have said something to or about a person that would cause that person hurt. This might involve something that the group members said to a friend or family member directly in anger, or it could be something they said behind those people's backs that would indirectly hurt them if they were to find out. They should be thinking about these situations as you move to the next step.

Option 2: Is It Gossip? For this option, you will need just this book. Read the following scenarios to the group and ask students to decide whether the character is involved in gossip or not.

- **Scenario #1:** I'm Gina. My friend told me she's thinking of running away, and I decided to tell my parents. Is this gossip? (*No, because you are acting in your friend's best interests. You are not gossiping if you are protecting someone. In addition, if you're telling someone's parents about something their kid is doing, it's usually not gossip.*)

- **Scenario #2:** Hi, Gina again. Now I want to tell my friends. Is this gossip? (*Yes, it's probably gossip because your motives for sharing the information are not just to help your friend.*)

- **Scenario #3:** Steven here. A guy in our youth group is drinking all the time. I told everyone so they could pray for him. Is this gossip? (*Probably. It's amazing how often Christians use the "prayer request excuse" for gossiping. Instead, you could ask for anonymous prayer by saying, "A person I know is drinking too much. I would like to pray that he or she would stop before it's too late."*)

- **Scenario #4:** It's me, Steven, again. I also emailed Sam and asked him to pray for that guy I told you about. I didn't tell Sam why or what the guy was doing. Is this gossip? (*Probably not. You could be even more careful by not mentioning the person's name and just say that it is a friend who needs prayer. After all, God knows the details!*)

- **Scenario #5:** Hey, I'm Christina. My friend called me and told me all these juicy stories about people in our school. I haven't repeated them to anyone, and don't even believe most of them. Is this gossip? (*Yes! Just by listening to gossip, you've given those who gossip more power. But if you tell them at the beginning of the conversation that you don't want to hear the gossip, you might at least stop some of it.*)

Conclude by asking the group to think of any times during the previous week when they found themselves in situations like these individuals. How did they respond? How should they have responded? They can be thinking about these situations as you move to the next step.

APPLY

Option 1: No Gossip Card #1. For this option, you will need several Bibles, index cards and pens or pencils. You can also write the words of James 1:26 on a large piece of butcher paper, poster board or on a white board.

Distribute the Bibles, index cards and pens or pencils. Ask the group members to think about the past week and ask themselves, *What is one time that I have been involved in gossip?* (They don't need to write anything down yet.)

Ask the group members to look up James 1:26 in their Bibles and rewrite the verse in their own words on the cards. Have them spend a few minutes thinking about what they would need to change so they would be able to keep better control of their tongues. When they think of changes they need to make, they should write them on the other side of the card. Let them know that by doing this, they will be making a commitment to God to try to enact this change.

Close in prayer, asking that God will give the group members the strength and wisdom to be able to make the needed changes. Instruct them to keep their cards as a reminder of their commitments to try to keep gossip out of their lives. Remember to follow-up with students in the upcoming weeks to see how they are doing in their commitments to avoid gossip.

Option 2: No Gossip Card #2. For this option you will need several Bibles, index cards and pens or pencils. You can also write the words of James 1:26 on a large piece of butcher paper, poster board or on a white board.

Distribute the Bibles, index cards and pens or pencils. Ask the group members to think about the past week and ask themselves, *What is one time I have been involved in gossip?* Note that they don't need to write anything down yet.

Ask the students to look up James 1:26 and rewrite the verse in their own words on the cards. Have them spend a few minutes thinking about what they would need to change so they would be able to keep better control of their tongues. Next, ask them to flip over the card and write down the name of one person they've gossiped with during the past week. Instruct them to circle that person's name if they would be willing to talk to him or her during the upcoming week about the commitment they have made to avoid gossiping.

If the group members are willing to make this additional commitment, have them write a sentence below the person's name to outline when and where they will speak with that individual. Close in prayer, asking God to open the hearts and minds of the people the students have listed on their cards so they might also be willing to make a commitment not to gossip. Remember to ask the group members in the weeks that come how they are doing in their commitments.

REFLECT

The following short devotions are for the group members to reflect on and answer during the week. You can make a copy of these pages and distribute to your class or download and print from **www.gospellight.com/uncommon/jh_dealing_with_pressure.zip.**

1—A MALICIOUS WITNESS

Let's talk about *talk.* Read Exodus 23:1.

It started out simple enough. Dave told Jeff that Sam liked Kim, and then Jeff told Danny. Danny misunderstood and told Robby that Sam had gone out with Kim, and Robby, trying to make the story more interesting, told the rest of the guys on the soccer team that Sam had kissed Kim. Finally, the story reached Kim's best friend, Suzy, who didn't believe any of it. She went straight to Kim and asked if it were true. Kim was shocked and angry. She couldn't believe that Sam would lie like that!

It wasn't Sam who had lied; it was everyone else involved. Some had lied on purpose, while the others had just misunderstood. Regardless, gossip is never good. It always hurts someone. The word "malicious" means to have a desire to cause harm to another person. How could gossip be considered malicious?

_____

_____

_____

Be careful what you say. Even though you may not have started a rumor you heard, if you participate in spreading it, you can hurt another person. So, the next time you hear something about someone else, let the news *stop* with you.

2—WATCH IT!

So, how strong is the power of your words? Read James 3:5 to find out.
Which of the following would be the toughest to guard?

- ☐ The White House
- ☐ Buckingham Palace in London
- ☐ Your action figure collection
- ☐ Your mouth

The answer is your mouth. Why? Because your mouth is something that you have to guard each and every day. And it doesn't take much for you to slip up and let your mouth get you into trouble.

According to James 3:5, is our tongue a large or small part of the body? Does that mean it is not important? Why or why not?

_____

_____

_____

We must watch what we say! Think of one way you can guard your lips today, and ask God to help you carry it out. Try out your idea, and see if it works!

3—GO TO THE SOURCE

Check out Matthew 12:34-37 to see why we should be saying only good things!

Long ago in the Wild West, people had to travel for miles before they came across a watering hole where they and their animals could get a drink. Sometimes, however, what they found was water full of minerals and contamination. They couldn't drink it, because it could kill them. The problem came from the source. No matter how much water flowed into the waterhole, if it came from a contaminated source, it was bad.

Jesus never tried to soften what he said. In Matthew 12:34-37, He said that evil people just can't say anything good. That's because the problem starts not in the mouth or even in the mind, but in a person's heart. When there is something bad inside a person—at the source—he or she will say bad things.

All Christians struggle with the words they say, which is why you need God to fix the source of the negative stuff that's in your heart. So take a moment and talk to God. Tell Him your struggles, and ask Him to help you make better choices. Begin right away to use your mouth for good and not bad!

4—SPEAK DIFFERENT WORDS

If you want to avoid some pain, hobble over to Proverbs 25:18.

What do you think would hurt the most?

- ❏ A piece of packing tape ripped off your arm . . . slowly
- ❏ Someone squeezing lemon juice into a paper cut on your finger
- ❏ Biting your tongue
- ❏ Getting toothpaste in your eye

Although Proverbs 25:18 doesn't talk about toothpaste or lemon juice, it does talk about being at the wrong end of a club, a sword or a sharp arrow. Then it compares hitting someone with one of these objects to *spreading lies* about another person. Talk about serious damage! Is there anyone whom you've hurt recently with your words? If so, what will you do to resolve the situation?

_____

_____

_____

Always remember it is never too late to tell someone you are sorry for hurting them with your words. It is also never too late to stop gossiping about others!

THE PRESSURE OF FRIENDSHIPS

THE BIG IDEA

When you treat others as Jesus has treated you, you will not only have true friendships but you will also change others for good.

SESSION AIMS

In this session, you will guide group members to (1) learn the difference between exclusive and inclusive groups of friends; (2) find out what kind of friendships Jesus wants them to have; and (3) choose to include outsiders into their group of friends.

THE BIGGEST VERSE

"Nobody should seek his own good, but the good of others" (1 Corinthians 10:24).

OTHER IMPORTANT VERSES

Leviticus 19:18; 1 Samuel 16:6-7; Matthew 7:1-2; 23:27; John 7:24; 17:14-19; 1 Corinthians 13:1-13; Philippians 2:1-11; Colossians 4:5-6

Note: Additional options and worksheets in 8¹/₂" x 11" format for this session are available for download at **www.gospellight.com/uncommon/jh_dealing_with_pressure.zip**.

STARTER

Option 1: Break Through. For this option, you will need a timekeeping device with a seconds indicator and room for your group members to move around.

Greet the students and select one volunteer, who will be "the Outsider," to stand with you while the remainder of the group stands shoulder-to-shoulder in a tight circle (for a group larger than 15 students, break into two circles or more). Ask the Outsider to stand near the circle, and tell him or her that when you say go, he or she should try to get to the center of the circle as the group members form the circle try to keep him or her out. Keep track of how many seconds it takes the Outsider to reach the inside of the circle. Repeat the exercise several times using a new Outsider to see who is the fastest at getting into the circle.

Introduce the session by explaining that sometimes the students will encounter groups at school that make it difficult to get into their inner circles. Or, they may find themselves participating in such a group that excludes outsiders. Today, they will be learning how to respond to these types of situations.

Option 2: Cliques. For this option, you will need one copy of "Cliques" (found on the next page) and a prize. Ahead of time, cut apart the four clique boxes on the handout. (If you have more than 45 students, make additional copies. If you have less than 20 students, use only two or three of the clique boxes.)

Greet the group members and divide them into teams of 8 to 10 people. Inform the teams that they are now "cliques," and everyone must stay with his or her assigned clique. (Note: Don't allow students to divide into actual cliques of their own within their assigned groups. Try to break up the usual cliques for this exercise.) Give each of the groups a clique box and instruct them to spend a few minutes reading and working on how their clique will act. Ask each clique to choose two of its members to be its representatives. These two will work as a team and will ask the other cliques questions so they can guess what the rules of that clique are.

Have each clique come to the front of the room. Give the representatives from the first clique three minutes to question the other cliques. Then give the representatives from the second clique a chance, and so on. When all the cliques have been questioned, let each team guess what the rules are for the other cliques. Award 100 points for every rule correctly identified. (Feel free to award partial credit if someone's guess is close but not exact.) The members of the clique being questioned must actively and fully answer all questions. Give bonus points to the clique that is being questioned, depending on how well members play their parts.

Clique A: **The Twitchies**
Rule 1:   You never speak without twitching your head to the right.
Rule 2:   You speak very, very quietly.
Rule 3:   You all love horses and can hardly say a sentence without mentioning a horse.
Rule 4:   You can't stand it when people cross their arms—none of you *ever* do that. If someone crosses his or her arms when speaking with you, you turn away.

Clique B: **The Movers**
Rule 1:   You cannot keep still, ever. You are all in constant movement.
Rule 2:   You speak loudly—VERY LOUDLY.
Rule 3:   You love M&M candies. Most of you are constantly mumbling, "M and M and M and M and M."
Rule 4:   You can't stand it when people ask you questions. When they do, you always roll your eyes and say, "If you must know . . ." before you answer.

Clique C: **The Snooties**
Rule 1:   You think you're better than everyone else and constantly put your finger under your nose as if you are trying to block a bad smell.
Rule 2:   You talk down to everyone as if they're little children. You all giggle when someone in your group does this to someone from another group.
Rule 3:   You love clothes and always ask people what brand they're wearing.
Rule 4:   You can't stand it when people look at you. You regularly snap, "Hey! Stop looking at us!"

Clique D: **The Grossies**
Rule 1:   You love to be gross—you burp and make rude noises all the time. (C'mon, get into it!)
Rule 2:   You snicker and laugh at everything.
Rule 3:   You love Jell-O and can't make it through a conversation without mentioning it.
Rule 4:   You can't stand it when people don't talk. If someone just stands there, you start groaning and shout, "Aren't you going to say something?!"

After the questioning is over, reveal the rules of each clique, and then discuss the following:

- What kinds of cliques exist in your school? (*Allow students to respond.*)
- What kinds of rules do the cliques at your school have? (*Certain cliques might expect them to wear a certain style of clothing, or talk a certain way, or be involved in a certain school activity or non-activity.*)
- Who creates the rules in a clique? (*Sometimes it's the whole group, though there are usually one or two influential people who decide most of the rules.*)
- What happens when a group member violates the clique's rules? (*The person is usually kicked out of the clique or at least harassed until he or she conforms.*)

Transition to the next step by explaining that because most of us deal with cliques every day, today we will be learning what God has to say about them.

MESSAGE

Option 1: A Different Kind of Love. For this option, you will need several Bibles and a few romantic greeting cards.

Begin by reading the greeting cards aloud, making sure to emphasize any mushy-gushy language. Next, distribute the Bibles to the group members and explain that the word in the Greek language for romantic love is *eros*. However, another word in the Greek language, *agape*, describes a completely different kind of love. *Agape* is the unconditional love that God has for each of us. He loves us no matter what we do or what we say or believe. He also wants us to have that kind of love for others. Paul describes this type of love in detail 1 Corinthians 13:1-13.[1]

Youth Leader Tip
Every junior-higher feels excluded at times. Be sensitive to these students in your group and add a time of prayer for this issue at the close of the session. Have some adults ready with open arms and listening ears.

Choose a volunteer to read the passage aloud, and then discuss the following questions as the group:

- Why is love such a big deal to God? (*He is unable to not love—in fact, He is love itself!*)

- How can you be part of a clique and still be loving to people? (*By not allowing the clique to exclude people or be mean to them.*)

- Is it possible to be popular and also practice what this passage talks about? (*It all depends on why you're popular. If you are popular because of your looks, your athletic ability or your wealth, then your popularity is based on temporary things—things you could easily lose! But if you are popular because you love others with God's* agape *love, then you are putting this passage into practice.*)

Read 1 Corinthians 10:24. Ask the group members what they think it means to seek "the good of others." (*The answer would be that the students will be kind to others and care about them. Other people's feelings and needs will matter to them.*) Next, read Philippians 2:1-11 aloud and discuss the following questions:

- Who is our model for putting others' needs before our own? (*Jesus.*)

- How did Jesus demonstrate that He put our needs before His own? (*He gave up everything to be our servant. He gave His very life to save us.*)

- Why is it so difficult to put other people's needs before our own? (*We tend to be selfish people who are more concerned about ourselves than we are about other people's needs and feelings.*)

Conclude by stating that when we truly have an attitude like Jesus, we will not consider ourselves to be above others. We will show others love and as a result we will include them in our friendships. Just as God has accepted us and brought us into His family, we need to reach the world with His love and compel others to follow Him.

Option 2: Coconuts or Oranges? For this option, you will need your Bible, a whole coconut, a whole orange, and a straight pin.

Begin by stating that *exclusive* cliques definitely have their down side—both for those in the clique (who are not showing God's love to others), and for those outside the clique (who will feel hurt that they have been shunned). In 1 Corinthians 13:1-13, Paul states that you can be the most popular and liked person in the world, but if you don't have love, you're worthless. (That's a *very* loose paraphrase!) This means that any group that is exclusive will be destructive to those who are excluded. Hold up the coconut, and tell the group that this represents an *exclusive* group. Try to stick the pin into it. Explain that a coconut has some really good stuff on the inside of it, but unless you can get through the outside, the inside is worthless. The same is true of exclusive groups.

Now state that *inclusive* cliques definitely have their up side—both for those in the clique (who feel close because they are part of a special group), and for those outside the clique (who will feel valued when they are allowed to join). We all need friendships with people on whom we can count, but in order to avoid becoming an exclusive clique, we must be open to allowing others to join our group. Hold up the orange, and tell the group that this represents an *inclusive* group. Stick the pin into it. Explain that like the coconut, an orange has a lot of good stuff on the inside; but unlike the coconut, the orange has an outside that allows easy access to the inside. The same is true of *inclusive* groups.

Conclude by stating it is this second type of group that we find in the book of Acts when the Early Church began. When people heard the gospel and accepted Jesus, they became part of an *inclusive* group of other believers. The members of these groups drew strength from each other, even in the face of persecution, and worked to share the gospel with those around them. In this way, these *inclusive* groups grew to thousands of believers within a short time.

Conclude by challenging the group members to begin including people who aren't accepted by other groups into their own circle of friends.

DIG

Option 1: Exclusive to Inclusive. For this option, you will need paper, pens or pencils and a room full of talkative students. Begin by discussing the following questions:

- Think of one exclusive (closed to outsiders) group at school. Are the members of that group ever mean to other people? If so, in what ways?
- Are there certain people in school that the group likes to tease or make fun of? If so, what types of people?
- Have you ever been the victim of this type of teasing? If so, how did it make you feel?

- Have you ever participated in making fun of someone who wasn't in your group? (This could be indirectly through gossip or even directly by making fun of the person.) If so, how do you think that person felt (or would feel if they found out you were talking about him or her)?
- How would an exclusive group react if one of its members tried to make it more loving and inclusive (open to outsiders)?
- Does your own group of friends tend to be more inclusive or exclusive?

Divide the students into groups of four to five people and distribute a piece of paper and a pen or pencil to each group. Give the groups two minutes to come up with ways they can make the group to which they belong at school (or church) more inclusive. Have the group that came up with the most ideas share its list first, and then have the other groups add anything that the first group may have missed.

Option 2: Jenna's Decision. For this option, you will need just this case study. Read the following aloud to the group:

Jenna wants to be a loving person—just as the Bible teaches. There certainly are lots of people in her school who could use a little love! But there's a problem: Jenna is included in a popular clique, and this particular group is mean to people outside of it. Jenna has tried to drop hints to her friends by saying things such as, "We don't have to be so mean to people," and, "Let's ask the new girl to hang out with us," but everyone just looks at her as if she's an alien when she says things like this. They continue to treat outsiders badly.

Now discuss the following questions with the group:

- What options does Jenna have? (*She could drop out of the clique; she could stay in the clique, continue to stick up for the ones being picked on, and walk away when the teasing won't stop; she could leave the clique and make friends with the people who are being picked on.*)
- What might these options cost her? (*She would no longer have an influence on the group; she might be kicked out of the group; she might become their next target.*)
- What might the reward be? (*Knowing that she is doing the right thing by modeling what God's love looks like; making some new and better friends.*)

- Knowing the possible cost to herself, what should Jenna do? (*She should do what Jesus would do!*)

Transition to the next step by stating that whenever we are part of a certain group of friends, we will be pressured to conform to the standards of that group. How we respond to that pressure will determine our integrity and whether or not we will serve as a light to others that will draw them to Christ.

APPLY

Option 1: My Clique. For this option, you will need copies of "My Clique" (found on the next page) and pens or pencils. Distribute the handout and pens or pencils to the group members and give them a few minutes to complete it. When everyone is finished, take a few minutes to discuss the responses. Talk about what the students think they should do to make their groups at school more loving and accepting of others, and then close in prayer, asking God to help them act on their ideas this week.

Option 2: Break Down the Walls. For this option, you will need index cards and pens or pencils. Begin by distributing the cards and writing instruments to the group members, and then ask them to think of a few people at their schools who seem unloved and excluded. They should write the initials of up to three of these people on their cards.

Tell the group members that they will now be spending a few minutes praying for the people they have listed on their cards. Instruct them to think about what these outsiders must be feeling when they are excluded from groups and then ask God for specific ways they can show love to these people this week and break down the walls that keep them out. Ask them to write any ideas that God gives to them on their cards.

After the personal prayer time is finished, gather everyone back together and ask the group members to keep the cards in a place where they will see them throughout the week (such as in a textbook, on the refrigerator, on their desk at home, and so forth). The cards will serve as a reminder for what they have decided to do for those individuals.

Close in prayer, asking God to help the group members find opportunities to reach out to outsiders they listed on their cards. Take some time during the week to contact the group members to see how they are doing with their plans. Encourage them in their efforts and offer any help or advice as needed.

MY CLIQUE

Think about one group of friends that you have. Using only their first names, who are the main people in this group?

_____
_____
_____
_____
_____

Are there other people who are sometimes accepted in this group, but are not considered apart of it? If so—again using only first names—who are they?

_____
_____
_____
_____
_____

Based on the following scale, how exclusive or inclusive is your group?

1	2	3	4	5	6	7	8	9	10

Totally exclusive	A little exclusive	A little inclusive	Totally inclusive
(No one can get in!)	(It isn't easy to get in)	(We try to be kind)	(We accept anyone)

What are five things you could do to help your group be more loving and accept a greater variety of people?

1. _____
2. _____
3. _____
4. _____
5. _____

Now, circle one of your answers that you're willing to work on this week!

REFLECT

The following short devotions are for the group members to reflect on and answer during the week. You can make a copy of these pages and distribute to your class or download and print from **www.gospellight.com/uncommon/jh_ dealing_with_pressure.zip**.

1—LOVE YOUR NEIGHBOR

How are you supposed to love your neighbor? Read Leviticus 19:18 to find out.

Annie and Lizzy had been neighbors for as long as they could remember. When they were younger, they played together every day, but as they grew up, they found that they had different interests and did not spend as much time together. Now they're in middle school. Annie hangs out with the girls who are into drama, and Lizzy hangs out with the skaters.

One day when Annie sat down to have lunch with her friends, she heard them ripping Lizzy apart! "She dresses like a boy and takes that dumb skateboard *everywhere*!" they said. Annie's friends giggled until they saw the look on her face. "Hey," Annie said, putting down her lunch, "just because Lizzy isn't into the same stuff as we are doesn't mean she isn't a cool person."

Do you think that Annie did the right thing? Why or why not?

_____

_____

_____

According to Leviticus 19:18, how are we to love our neighbors? What do you think that means?

_____

_____

_____

"Loving your neighbor" doesn't mean loving just the people who live next door. Your neighbors include all the people you meet in life. This includes the kids on the school bus, the guy who eats lunch alone, and the girl with the funny glasses. What are two ways you can show love to these types of people today?

_____

_____

_____

2—INSIDE OR OUTSIDE?

What does God consider when He looks at a person? Read 1 Samuel 16:6-7 to find the answer.

Samuel was an important prophet of the Old Testament, but even he got things wrong at times. Such was the case when he went to pick the next king of Israel. Samuel saw Eliab, and he was so impressed with the young man that he thought, "Surely the LORD's anointed stands here." He made his choice based on the outside, but God made His choice based on the inside of the person—and He chose David to be the next king.

Do you usually choose your friends because of the way they dress, how they act, or for their personalities?

_____

_____

_____

Why is it hard to look past outward appearances when considering your friends?

_____

_____

_____

How comfortable are you with people from other groups?

_____

_____

_____

Look again at what God says in 1 Samuel 16:7: "The LORD does not look at the things man looks at. Man looks at the outward appearance, but the LORD looks at the heart." Today, pray that God would help you see people as they really are—which is way more important than what they wear or how they look.

3—BACKING OUT

Read John 7:24 and fill in the blanks:

Stop _____ by mere _____, and make a _____ judgment.

Ian was an impressive guy. He wore expensive blue jeans, T-shirts with the names of his favorite bands on them, and only the best shoes. And he only talked to people who wore nice clothes like him.

One day in gym class, Ian was wearing his dorky gym clothes (just like everyone else) when he ran into a guy named Jack. The two hit it off, and Ian invited Jack to come to his youth group. But after class, Ian saw that Jack had changed into clothes that weren't as nice as his. In fact, they were a little shabby.

Ian liked Jack, but he grew concerned that being seen around him would damage his reputation. So, the next day in gym class, he made up an excuse to get out of inviting Jack to his youth group.

Look up Matthew 7:1-2. What was wrong with the way Ian was treating Jack?

_____

_____

_____

What does God say about those who judge others?

_____

_____

_____

If Ian wanted to do the right thing, what would he need to change?

_____

_____

_____

Maybe you have been guilty of judging people the way Ian did. If so, you might be cutting yourself off from some great people! Just because someone doesn't fit the exact mold of someone you would normally choose to have as a friend doesn't mean that he or she wouldn't be a great friend. So be kind to everyone you meet today. Who knows? Maybe you'll make some new friends.

4—EVERYONE IS WATCHING

Turn on the lights and go read Matthew 5:14-16.

If you wanted to light up your house, the last thing you would do is take a lamp and put it under a bowl. Instead, you would put it up high so that the light lit up the greatest amount of space. This is why lights are on the ceilings instead of on the floors.

The same is true of us. As Christians, we should be reflecting God's light, not hiding it. Our actions should point others to God and show that we serve Him. To do this, we have to accept others and make them a part of our group.

If you were somewhere with a group of friends from your youth group, what would the other people sitting around you see, hear or think about your group?

_____
_____
_____
_____

Do you think that the people around you would know you were Christians? Why or why not?

_____
_____
_____
_____

A flashlight that flickers off and on is useless (and a bit annoying). So let your light for Jesus shine strongly. Don't have a life-light that is sometimes bright and sometimes off. Point others to Christ by shining your light on the path that leads to heaven.

TOP 10 PRESSURES A JUNIOR-HIGHER WILL FACE

In this unit, we've looked at a number of different pressures your group members will face at school, at home and with their friends. There is no doubt that teens today face all kinds of stressors that have an impact on their mental, physical, emotional and spiritual health. But what are the *top* pressures they will face? While the opinions from experts differ to some degree, here are what many consider to be the 10 most critical stressors a young person will encounter.

1. Body Image: Today, kids are bombarded with images in the media of what the "ideal" person should look like. Trying to measure up to this impossible standard can cause a great deal of stress in a young person's life.

2. Acceptance by Peers: Everyone wants to be liked, and this is especially true of junior-highers. Not feeling accepted by others can be a high cause of stress.

3. The Opposite Sex: There is tremendous pressure today for young people to have sex, and many give in so they will feel accepted and part of the "in" crowd.

4. Drugs and Alcohol: Movies and music aimed toward young people often glorify drugs and alcohol. This can cause a lot of pressure for those who want to stand up for God and resist the temptation to do what all of their friends are likely doing.

5. Bullying: The problems with bullying have gained increased media attention in recent years. Adding to the stress is that bullying today doesn't occur only at school but also on social media sites, through text messages and in blogs.

6. College: With the increase in enrollment at universities in recent years, there is an increased pressure on students to keep their grades high so they can get into a good college. In addition, many colleges look for applicants who have done extracurricular activities and volunteer work. This pressure to achieve can trickle down to junior-highers and leave them with little down time to relax.

7. Personal Tragedy: Crises such as the death of a loved one, an illness of a friend or a divorce in the family are sources of stress in everyone's life regardless of age, but young people often have fewer tools they can use to cope with the tragedy.

8. Sports: Not only are junior-highers enrolled in more sports programs today, but also there is increased pressure to succeed and win in a competition. This increased pressure can cause a young person to lose interest in a sport he or she once enjoyed playing.

9. Financial Pressures: Financial stress begins for preteens and teenagers. Hanging out with friends, buying name brand clothing and paying for music and athletic gear all require money, and young people can get caught up in worrying about how they will pay for everything they want.

10. Growing Up: As children enter the adolescent years, they naturally assume more responsibilities. This transition time can create a lot of stress in a young person's life.[1]

These pressures are very real, and they can lead to a lot of negative consequences in your group members' lives. So today, make sure they know that they can take each of these issues—and anything else they are facing—to God in prayer. Remind them of these words from Christ: "Therefore I tell you, do not worry about your life, what you will eat or drink; or about your body, what you will wear. Is not life more important than food, and the body more important than clothes? Look at the birds of the air; they do not sow or reap or store away in barns, and yet your heavenly Father feeds them. Are you not much more valuable than they?" (Matthew 6:25-26).

UNIT II

Dealing with Change

During my many years of ministry to junior-highers, the topic of change confused me. That is, until I realized that when you add change to junior-highers, you get an antinomy. No, I'm not talking about a creature in the sea (that's a sea *anemone*). And I'm also not referring to a lack of red blood cells (that's *anemia*). An *antinomy* is a perceived, or real, contradiction between two equally true facts. The Christian faith is spiced with many antinomies: predestination and free will, Jesus as fully God and fully human, the benefits of junior-high retreats and the advantages of a good night of sleep—and, believe it or not, change and junior-highers.

Let me explain. On the one hand, it is true that there is no such thing as a junior-higher *not* changing. Beyond the more obvious physical, emotional and social changes, they are experiencing perpetual spiritual changes. (Actually, we *all* are.) As M. Robert Mulholland explains:

> Life is, by its very nature, spiritual formation. The question is not *whether* to undertake spiritual formation; the question is *what kind* of spiritual formation are we engaged in. Are we being increasingly conformed to the world, or are we being increasingly conformed to the image of Christ?[1]

If Mulholland is right—and I believe he is—there is no such thing as a student or a ministry that is not changing. The key question is the direction of the change. Yet just as it's true that junior-highers are always changing, it's equally true that *sometimes* change in an individual student is so slow it's *barely visible*. When I am asked to identify my favorite part of working with junior-highers, it's a no-brainer: I enjoy seeing them change. Yet as I look at my ongoing ministry with them, sometimes I go a long time without seeing many results. That's why the following illustration is something I like to remind myself of and to share with all junior-high youth workers within earshot.

A 10-year-old boy lived near the shore of Australia—so close that he could see the waves crash onto the beach from his bedroom window. The starfish particularly fascinated him. Every morning, the tide washed hundreds of them onto the warm sand, but then the same waves picked them up and carried them back into the ocean.

One particular Saturday, the boy peered out the window and found that something had gone terribly wrong. As the tide receded, there were hundreds of starfish left on the dry sand. The boy knew they would die if he didn't do something, so he raced out of his house and down to where they starfish lay. He picked up the first one he saw and tossed it into the ocean, and then picked up the next and tossed that one into the ocean. He kept doing this for every starfish he found.

His neighbor couldn't help but notice what the little boy was doing. He sauntered out of his kitchen, down to the beach, and stood next to the boy. "You're never going to get all of these starfish into the water before they die," he said. "Do you really think what you're doing is going to make a difference?"

"I don't know," the boy replied, picking up the next starfish. "But I do know it makes a difference to *this* one."

And he threw it into the water.

Kara Powell
Executive Director of the Fuller Youth Institute
Assistant Professor of Youth, Family and Culture
Fuller Theological Seminary

CHANGES IN OUR THINKING

THE BIG IDEA

We need to ask God to change us into the people He wants us to be, and that change begins in our minds.

SESSION AIMS

In this session, you will guide group members to (1) recognize their need for God to change their minds; (2) open their lives to God so He can change and transform them; and (3) commit to seeking and following God's will to change them through the choices that they make.

THE BIGGEST VERSES

"Therefore, I urge you, brothers, in view of God's mercy, to offer your bodies as living sacrifices, holy and pleasing to God—this is your spiritual act of worship. Do not conform any longer to the pattern of this world, but be transformed by the renewing of your mind" (Romans 12:1-2).

OTHER IMPORTANT VERSES

Joshua 1:8; Matthew 5:44; Luke 3:10-14; John 3:16; Romans 3:23; 5:8; 6:23; 8:5-6; Hebrews 3:12-13; 1 John 1:9; 3:16-18; 4:8

Note: Additional options and worksheets in 8^1/$_2$" x 11" format for this session are available for download at **www.gospellight.com/uncommon/jh_dealing_with_pressure.zip**.

STARTER

Option 1: The Collector. For this option, you will need one roll of masking tape for each team of students and a food prize for the winning team.

Welcome the group members and divide them into teams. Have each team choose one person to be "the Collector," and then give each team one roll of masking tape. Explain that in this game, you will be calling out certain items (some ideas include hair accessories, watches, socks, school ID cards, shoelaces and coins). The team members must look through their pockets and purses to collect as many of the items that you have called out as they can. Once the have found the item, they will need to use the masking tape to secure the items to the Collector.

The team with the most items collected and secured in each round will earn five points. Each round should last approximately three minutes. Award the food prize to the team that has the most points at the end of the game.

As the winning team is enjoying the victory prize, explain that in this game, the goal was to win the food prize. For the losing team, it probably isn't very rewarding right now for them to watch someone else enjoying what they would like to have. Life is the same way—we often get upset over things that we want but can't have.

Continue by stating that each of us has something called a "sin nature." This often causes us to focus on ourselves instead of others as the Bible commands, and it tempts us to make choices that don't please God. Each day, we are bombarded with temptations to make self-focused choices instead of God-focused choices. For this reason, it is important for us to distinguish between the two. This involves a change in our way of thinking, which we will discuss in this session.

Option 2: Take What You Can Get. For this option, you will need several different game items such as an inner tube, a Frisbee, a handball and a stuffed animal. You will also need a roll of masking tape, four plastic road cones and prizes—and maybe even an adult volunteer or two. Ahead of time, set up a 20' x 20' square area using the cones as the corner markers. Place the game items in the middle of the area. Tape a "safe" line at each corner and put the plastic cone in the middle of it.

Welcome the group members and ask all the guys to go to the left side of the room and the girls to go to the right side of the room. Have each guy number off aloud, "1, 2, 1, 2," and so on. Have each girl number off aloud, "3, 4, 3, 4," and so on. Ask all the guys who are a #1 to form a team, and have the

#2s do the same. Ask all the girls who are a #3 to form a team, and have the #4s do the same. Have team #1 and team #3 switch places, and then have everyone stand behind their safe line and plastic cone. Once a team member is in this safe area, a person from another team cannot touch that person or take his or her things.

Tell the group members that when you call their team's number, they are to run to the center of the square and to bring back as much "stuff" as they can to their corner. Each person can take only one thing at a time. No item is safe until a player crosses his or her team's safe line, which means that tug-of-wars will abound. (Note: It is best to keep the guys and the girls separated during this game, so make sure that you only have team #1 going against team #2 or team #3 going against #4.)

Play as many rounds as time and energy will allow. Keep track of the amount of items each team takes in each round and then return the items to the square. At the end of the game, add all of the teams' scores and award the prize to the team with the highest overall score. Have everyone come back together as a group, and then discuss the following questions:

- Did any of you get into a tug-of-war over the items? (*Most likely yes.*)
- Why did this happen? (*Each person wanted that item for his or her team.*)
- Did anybody on your team decide to help another team, such as by giving an opponent your stuff? (*Most likely no.*)
- Why didn't you help the other team? (*You knew that you wouldn't be able to win if you did that. You wouldn't get any prize.*)
- What are some real-life examples of stuff that people buy and keep for themselves, regardless of the fact that someone else might need it more? (*Money, clothes, cars, food and so on.*)
- What would you call this kind of behavior? (*Greed, selfishness.*)

Ask the group members if any of them have ever been guilty of putting their needs above the needs of others. (*If they are honest, everyone will say yes.*) The truth is that all of us are capable of selfishness and greed at times. This is because of something called the "sin nature." Human beings are self-centered, and it is this self-centeredness that causes us to make selfish choices against what God wants for our lives. However, as we mature in our relationship with Jesus, we will learn how to tell the difference between these self-centered choices and God-centered decisions. This requires a change in our way of thinking, which is the focus of today's session.

MESSAGE

Option 1: To Be a Butterfly. For this option, you will need several Bibles and a spray bottle filled with water. Choose 13 volunteers to act out a drama. Assign the following roles: a caterpillar; two butterflies, a great oak tree (three students), two leaves, two flowers, two tall blades of grass and the wind. (Note: If you don't have a large group, assign more than one role per person.)

Tell the group members that as you narrate the story, the volunteers will act out exactly what you say. Instruct the flowers to kneel down on one side of the great oak tree and have the tall blades of grass stand on the other side. The caterpillar, butterflies, leaves and the wind are offstage until you call upon them. Now narrate the story, pausing where indicated to allow your volunteers to perform the actions:

Once upon a time there was a caterpillar who was so sad that he was moaning to himself, *Woe is me* [pause] and, *I'm just a plain old caterpillar* [pause] as he crawled through the legs of the tall blades of grass [pause], who were swaying back and forth from the wind [pause].

Two beautiful butterflies came flying through [pause] the tall blades of grass and landed on the flowers [pause], laughing and bouncing up and down where they landed. When the caterpillar saw that the butterflies were so happy, he began to cry [pause] and sob [pause] and then wail uncontrollably [pause], until he finally had to blow his little caterpillar nose on the tall blades of grass [pause].

The butterflies noticed the caterpillar and flew over to see what was wrong [pause]. "What's wrong, caterpillar?" they asked in unison [pause]. Between sobs, the caterpillar replied, "I want to be beautiful like *you*! I wish I could change [pause]." And he sobbed some more [pause].

The butterflies laughed and laughed [pause]. They said in unison, "You can't change yourself. Only God can change you. Be patient and wait for Him." The caterpillar grew angry [pause] and whined, "I don't want to wait! I want to change right *now*!" With that, he stomped his little caterpillar feet [pause].

The butterflies laughed so hard that they fell to the ground [pause]. The caterpillar left the butterflies rolling around on the ground [pause] and crawled toward the great oak tree, who was looking sad and depressed [pause] and shaking his head. "I'll show those dumb flies I can change myself," the caterpillar mumbled to himself as he reached the great oak tree [pause].

The caterpillar picked up two leaves and announced, "These will be my new wings" [pause]. Taking the leaves in his little caterpillar hands, he climbed up onto the branches of the great oak tree [pause]. He could feel the wind in his little caterpillar face [pause], and he could even feel a little mist in the air [squirt the actor with the water].

The caterpillar, proud of his new wings, yelled out, "I'm a butterfly! I'm a butterfly! I'm a butterfly!" With that, he jumped off the great oak tree [pause], landing right onto the flowers. Discouraged and sore [pause], the Caterpillar decided that the butterflies were right. He climbed back up the great oak tree [pause] and started to build his cocoon, trusting that God would transform him into the beautiful butterfly that He intended him to be. The end.

Ask the group members why the caterpillar couldn't become a butterfly once he found some leaves for wings. Explain that even though he sort of looked like a butterfly on the outside, he wasn't truly changed on the inside. In the same way, there are people who say they are Christians but don't act like Jesus. Sometimes this is because nothing has really happened inside them. They are Christians in name only. They have not allowed Jesus to transform and change them on the inside.

Distribute the Bibles and explain that in the first five chapters of Romans, Paul describes how the Holy Spirit can work in and through us to help us to live in a way that pleases God. Choose a volunteer to read Romans 12:1-2 and 8:5-6 aloud.[1] Explain that even after we've asked Jesus to take over our lives, it's not always easy for us to live in the way that the Bible instructs us to live. Each day, we must decide between following our sinful nature and asking the Holy Spirit to help us seek God's will. If the Spirit is in control, He will help us make godly choices.

Choose a volunteer to read Joshua 1:8. State that it is our responsibility to study and memorize God's Word, to seek Him every day, and to allow the Holy Spirit to guide us in each and every decision we make. This is how God transforms our minds, and as we go through this transformation, we begin to resemble Jesus and act and behave in a way that pleases Him.

Option 2: It Takes a Little Pressure. For this option, you will need several Bibles (a *New Living Translation* if possible), a tablespoon-sized measuring spoon, cornstarch, water, small paper cups, plastic spoons, a newspaper and a detailed picture that you can show in a way that the entire group will be able to see it.

Ahead of time, prepare the following set of items for each group of three to five students: one paper cup with one tablespoon water, one paper cup with two tablespoons cornstarch, a plastic spoon, and two sheets of newspaper.

Also ahead of time, read through this option and practice using the ingredients. Rehearse applying pressure to the mixture to make it solidify and removing pressure to make it liquefy. Also experiment with the ratios—for example, you may want to use a higher cornstarch-to-water ratio during the actual demonstration.

Begin by reading Romans 12:2 to the group members (from the *New Living Translation* if possible). Explain that the phrase "let God transform you" means that it is God who needs to make the necessary changes in us—we can't change on our own. So, how does God do this? First, He does so through the influence of the Holy Spirit. Choose a volunteer to read Romans 8:5-6 (from the *New Living Translation* if possible). Explain that when we are led by our sinful nature, we will think about sinful things; but if we allow the Holy Spirit to control us, we will think about the things that please God.

Divide group members into teams of three to five people and distribute the sets of ingredients to each group. Instruct the group members to slowly add the water to the cornstarch, but not to stir it yet. If they follow your instructions, the mixture in their cup will remain in liquid form. Show the entire group your liquid mixture. Explain that just as the liquid can't become solid on its own, neither can we change our sinful nature without the Holy Spirit working in us.

Now ask the group members to stir their mixtures. They will soon figure out that they can't stir the mixture very easily, because it hardens with pressure. Pour some of the mixture into your hand and apply pressure to show how it changes into a solid substance. Continue by stating that the same is true for us. When we allow the Holy Spirit to work in our lives and to apply pressure where needed, God will change us on the inside. As we change on the inside, we will begin to reflect Christ to others.

Conclude by stating that a second way God changes us is through His Word. Choose a volunteer to read Joshua 1:8. Explain that just as Joshua instructed the Israelites to "study this Book of Instruction [the Bible] continually" (*NLT*), we are to seek God through His Word continually. As we do—and as we allow the Holy Spirit to guide us in every decision we make—our hearts and our minds are transformed. When this occurs, we will look very different than we did before. Our lives will be a blessing to others because we are no longer focused on our own interests, and we will be able to reflect God's glory.

DIG

Option 1: A Lesson in Prayer. For this option, you need a copy of "A Lesson in Prayer" (found on the next page) and a female volunteer to act out the monologue. Ahead of time, give the handout to the volunteer to practice her lines.

Introduce the monologue to the group. After the award-winning performance, discuss the following questions:

- What were the differences in these three prayers to God?
- Which prayer do you think God would want us to pray? Why?

Explain that this performance showed us a great example of how to spend time with God and listen to the Holy Spirit's guidance when we are seeking to do His will. We have to spend time with God to have Him give us the right mental perspective so we know what to pray.

Option 2: Harley's Prayer. For this option, you will need paper and pens or pencils for every three or four group members. Begin by sharing the following case study:

Harley got up early this morning and rushed into the shower to get ready for school. Today was a big day. He was going to ask Danielle to go with him to the party Friday night.

Before breakfast, Harley took some time to read his Bible and talk with God. He came across 1 Corinthians 10:13, in which Paul states that God will not allow us to be tempted beyond what we can bear, and that He will always gives a way out if we are tempted.

Harley knows he's been blowing it lately. He's been struggling at school, especially in world history. He's been copying Danielle's history homework during math—he even cheated off her paper yesterday during a pop-quiz. He really likes Danielle, but the guys at school are pressuring him to take their relationship to a physical level that he knows is wrong. To top it all off, Harley has been fighting with his best friend, Jeff, and has been talking behind Jeff's back.

With this in mind, Harley begins his prayer to God for the day ahead of him.

Divide the group members into teams of three to four people. Distribute paper and pens or pencils and instruct the group members to write a prayer for

A Lesson in Prayer

(Note: Begin by reading this prayer very formally, but then get more casual when you start speaking about the basketball team. Follow the directions given in the text.)

Dear Lord, thank You for this day. Thank You for Your grace and mercy. Thank You for always being with us (*pause*).

Lord, today I ask You to please, please, *please* let me make the basketball team—(*quickly adding in*) and let me beat out Laura Gillespe. Lord, You know everything, so you know that Laura gets everything she wants. She's president of our class, she was in the school play, and I don't think she even *wants* to be on the team. I, on the other hand, *really* want to be on the team. Would it be so bad if I could get something instead of her once in a while?

Actually, Lord, I think it would be a good lesson in humility for her *not* to get picked. I was just reading in my devotional book how we should be humble. And if someone needs to learn that lesson, it's *Laura*! She needs to learn that we are all equal and we shouldn't consider ourselves better than others. (*Pause.*) Yeah! (*Pause.*) Oh . . . I guess that applies to me too. Lord, can I take that all back? Here, let's start again . . .

(*Speaking formally again.*) Dear Lord, thank You for this day. Thank You for Your grace and mercy. Thank You for always being with us (*pause*). (*More casual again.*) Lord, please, please, *please* let me make the basketball team. You know everything, so You know that I want to be on this team more than anything. I've worked so hard for it. Well . . . at least I've been working hard for it since last week, when I overheard Bobby Phillips say he likes girls who play sports. So, I guess I haven't worked *that* hard, but I still want to make the team.

Actually, Lord, I think this would be a great opportunity for me to learn how to work with others. It would be great to be on a team with a coach, going to practices and running all those drills . . . (*pauses*). Wow, that could be a lot of work. It's going to take a lot of effort for me to succeed on a team. I guess I shouldn't just expect things to be handed to me. Hmm. Lord, can I start over one more time?

Dear Lord, thank You for today and for everything I've learned. As you know, basketball tryouts are today, so please be with Coach Jones as she chooses the best girls for the team. And, Lord, could You be with all the girls who are trying out, whether they make it or not?

Thank You for taking the time to be with me. Amen.

Harley. Note that they should write it for this day only. Allow a few minutes for them to write the prayer, and then discuss the following questions:

- How can God make a difference in Harley's choices? (*Some answers include He will help Harley to resist the temptation to cheat, He will help him to stop gossiping about his friend, and He will give him the strength to stand up to the pressure of the guys at school.*)

- Will Harley become perfect if he prays? (*Sure! And we've got some banana groves in Siberia we're sellin' cheap!*)

- So, what's the point? (*We are a work in progress. Transformation doesn't happen overnight; it's a lifelong process.*)

Conclude by explaining that while we're always going to have ups and downs, if we continually turn our lives over to God and ask for His strength, we will find that our lives will change and God will help us to make good choices. Our goal is to continually look to God as our source of strength and to ask Him to transform us each and every day.

APPLY

Option 1: Top 10 Temptations. For this option, you will need a whiteboard, a whiteboard marker, paper and pens or pencils. Ahead of time, write the following items on the whiteboard:

1. Cursing
2. Gossiping
3. Lying
4. Talking back to your parents or other adults
5. Drinking alcohol
6. Doing drugs or smoking
7. Yelling at or hitting a brother or sister
8. Stealing
9. Looking at R-rated or X-rated Internet sites
10. Cheating

Explain to the group that one of the reasons we tend to make bad choices is because we don't decide ahead of time what we're going to do when we're faced with new situations and options. State that now that the group members are middle-schoolers, they will be confronting new situations all the time—situations that will require them to choose the right response.

Distribute the paper and pens or pencils. Read the list from the whiteboard to the group, and then explain that these are some of the common temptations that junior-highers typically face. Instruct the group members to write down any of the items that they have been tempted with recently, and then have them circle the three temptations they face most often. Next to the circled temptations, ask them to write down the way they think God would like them to respond the next time those temptations occur.

Allow a few minutes for the group members to write down their answers. When they are finished, challenge them to place a star next to any of the temptations that they are willing to stand against this week. Remind them to continue to ask God for His help in every decision and for Him to help them to stand strong in the face of temptation.

Option 2: Big Thoughts. For this option, you need copies of "Big Thoughts" (found on the next page) and pens or pencils. Begin by explaining that people come to know Jesus as their Savior at different times and in different places, but regardless of how people find Christ, it basically comes down to three things: (1) faith, (2) feelings and (3) facts. While we have little control over people's faith or feelings, we can help them get to know Jesus by presenting the facts. We do this by sharing the gospel in a way that makes sense to them and helps them understand the truth about Jesus.

Distribute the "Big Thoughts" handouts and pens or pencils. Instruct the group members to number the Scripture verses in order of how they would use them to share their faith with someone else. In other words, ask them to list which verses they would share first to bring people to a place where they acknowledge their sins and their need for a Savior, and which verses would work best to lead individuals through the process.

Allow three minutes for the group members to order their lists. When time is up, choose a few volunteers to share their order and why they chose it. Next, challenge the group members to each circle one verse they would like to share with others and memorize this week. (Remember to invite the group members to share their verses next week and have prizes available to reward them.)

Close in prayer, thanking God for the guidance of the Holy Spirit and asking Him to continue to help the group members to make decisions in their lives that honor and please Him.

BIG THOUGHTS

Number these verses from 1 to 6 in the order you would use them to share about your relationship with Jesus with someone else.

☐ "For God so loved the world that he gave his one and only Son, that whoever believes in Him shall not perish but have eternal life" (John 3:16).

☐ "For all have sinned and fall short of the glory of God" (Romans 3:23).

☐ "But God demonstrates his own love for us in this: While we were still sinners, Christ died for us" (Romans 5:8).

☐ "For the wages of sin is death, but the gift of God is eternal life in Christ Jesus our Lord" (Romans 6:23).

☐ "If we confess our sins, he is faithful and just and will forgive us our sins and purify us from all unrighteousness" (1 John 1:9).

☐ "Whoever does not love does not know God, because God is love" (1 John 4:8).

REFLECT

The following short devotions are for the group members to reflect on and answer during the week. You can make a copy of these pages and distribute to your class or download and print from **www.gospellight.com/uncommon/jh_dealing_with_pressure.zip**.

1—SETTING AN EXAMPLE

How should we be living? Read Hebrews 3:12-13 to find out.

Imagine you hear that one of your church friends went to a party and drank some beer—quite a bit, in fact. You've heard a few other things lately that make you wonder what's going on with this friend. What do you do?

- ❐ Stop talking to your friend.
- ❐ Tell everyone at church to stay away from your friend.
- ❐ Talk to your friend privately, asking if the rumors are true and how you can help him or her make better choices.
- ❐ Start going to parties with your friend.

Underage drinking is against the law, but many young people do it anyway. Why do you think Christians—who know better—sometimes go ahead and do what is wrong?

_____

_____

_____

The author of Hebrews tells us to live in a way that pleases God and to encourage others to do the same. So, when we see our friends sinning, we need to set an example and not join in what they are doing. Even more, we need to care about them enough to encourage them to make better choices. Today, take a moment to think about what you can say to a friend who is struggling with sin. What will you do to show Christ's love for that person?

2—HELPING THOSE IN NEED

How does God want us to treat those who are in need? Read Luke 3:10-14.

Jenny was walking downtown with her mother when they saw a woman huddled at a bus stop. It was cold outside, and the woman had no coat. She looked as if she might be homeless. Suddenly, Jenny's mother stopped and went back to the bus stop. She took off her coat and gave it to the woman.

"Mom, why did you give that woman your new coat?" Jenny asked.

"Well, Jenny," her mother replied, "the Bible says we're supposed to love other people in the same way that we love ourselves. We are supposed to take care of the poor. That woman had no coat, so I gave her mine. I can get another one for myself. I believe it is what Jesus wanted me to do."

In Luke 3:11, what did John the Baptist tell the crowd they should do?

_____

_____

_____

In verses 12-14, what did he tell the tax collectors to do? What did he tell the soldiers to do?

_____

_____

_____

_____

John's words to the people required them to change the way they thought about the poor. Today, how do you need God to change your thinking?

3—PUTTING OTHERS FIRST

What is the greatest act of love ever? Read 1 John 3:16-18 to find out.

Imagine that your friends have invited you to go to a concert a few hours away. You're going to drive there together and be gone all day. It's going to be great! But then, 30 minutes before you're supposed to leave, you go to the living room and see that your little brother is crying. Your mom tells you he is sad because he thinks no one likes him or wants to be his friend. He looks up at you and says, "Don't leave. I want to play with you!" What do you do?

- ❏ Tell your brother you have the rest of your lives to hang out with him, but this concert is a-once-in-a-lifetime experience.
- ❏ Call your friends and tell them to go to the concert without you.
- ❏ Offer to take your brother to the concert.
- ❏ Play with him for 30 minutes, then sneak out when he's not looking.

Laying down your life for someone doesn't always mean dying or becoming a hero. It means doing something kind for another person, even though it might cost you time, money, work or doing what they want to do rather than doing what you want to do. This requires a change in your thinking! When was a time that you were completely unselfish? How did it feel?

_____

_____

_____

Today, pray about the areas of your life where you might be making selfish choices. Ask God to help you to choose to be unselfish this week.

4—CHANGING HOW WE LOOK AT ENEMIES

How are we to treat our enemies? Read Matthew 5:44.

Wendy and Josh did *not* get along, to put it mildly. One day, Wendy was running and some money fell out of her pocket. When Josh saw the cash fall out, he jumped on it before she realized what had happened. *This will get her back for that time she was mean to me,* he thought. Just as he began to put the money in his pocket, he remembered something he had learned at church: "Love your enemies and pray for those who persecute you." He began to think about how he would feel if he had lost the money. He knew he would want it back.

John knew what he needed to do. He walked back to over to where Wendy was sitting. "Hey, you dropped this," he said, placing the money on the table.

It's not easy to love our enemies. We would rather scratch their eyes out, especially if they treat us badly. But remember: even though Jesus was treated badly, He loved us so much that He willingly suffered and died for our sins.

Think about your "enemies"—those people who just seem to irritate you at times. What does Matthew 5:44 tell you to do for those people?

_____

_____

_____

_____

Praying for our enemies and not getting even with them when they make us mad requires a change in our thinking. But with God's help we can do it. And who knows—maybe that person will end up being a friend!

CHANGES IN OUR RELATIONSHIPS WITH THE OPPOSITE SEX

THE BIG IDEA

As our thoughts and feelings for the opposite sex change, we need to understand that God created our emotions and put those feelings inside of us.

SESSION AIMS

In this session, you will guide group members to (1) learn what God says about relationships with the opposite sex; (2) understand that God wants them to treat the opposite sex with respect in the same way they would like to be treated; and (3) choose to treat the opposite sex in a respectful and godly way.

THE BIGGEST VERSES

"A new command I give you: Love one another. As I have loved you, so you must love one another. By this all men will know that you are my disciples, if you love one another" (John 13:34-35).

OTHER IMPORTANT VERSES

Genesis 2; Leviticus 19:18; Deuteronomy 6:4-5; Proverbs 21:23; 24:17-18; Ecclesiastes 3:1; Matthew 7:12; Mark 12:28-31; John 13:14; Romans 12:10; 15:7; Galatians 5:13; 6:2; Ephesians 4:32; 1 John 4:7

Note: Additional options and worksheets in 8$\frac{1}{2}$" x 11" format for this session are available for download at **www.gospellight.com/uncommon/jh_dealing_with_pressure.zip**.

STARTER

Option 1: Close Shave. For this option, you will need several long balloons, several round balloons, shaving cream, two disposable razors, and a small prize. Ahead of time, blow up one balloon of each size.

Welcome the group members and choose two volunteers (a guy and a girl) to come forward. Explain that the volunteers are going to be practicing their shaving skills—the guy is going to shave his leg and the girl is going to shave her face! When your volunteers start to panic, tell them they will be using balloons. Give the round (face-shaped) balloon to the girl, and give the long (leg-shaped) balloon to the guy. Apply the shaving cream to each balloon and give the volunteers their razors. Signal for the volunteers to begin. The first one to finish shaving his or her balloon is the winner. (Note: if one of the balloons pops, the remaining contestant wins.)

Award the prize to the winner, and then explain that as junior-highers, they are going through many changes—with shaving likely being one of them. In addition, they might have noticed that the way they think and feel about the opposite sex has also changed. Members of the opposite sex are no longer creepy creatures they run away from screaming. Today, the group is going to learn how God wants them to treat each other, especially as they begin to think about each other differently.

Option 2: Who Knows Best? For this exercise, you need the multiple-choice questions listed below and some prizes. Begin by welcoming the students, and then divide the group members by gender. Ask the guys to go to the left side of the room and the girls to go to the right side. Explain that today you are going to give them the chance to prove who knows more about the opposite sex—boys or girls. Pause for the oohs and ahhs, and then explain the rules:

1. You (the leader) will read a set of multiple-choice questions that each side will get a chance to answer.

Youth Leader Tip
Video interviews can be an effective way to illustrate and communicate. One bonus is that if you go to your local school (off campus) to do the interviews, you can invite the students to come and check out your youth group!

2. You will be alternating the questions between the two sides, with each side getting one question at a time.
3. When it is one team's turn, the other team can't make any noise at all, or they will lose a point.
4. The teams must clap for the answer they think is correct.

Begin the game, awarding 10,000 points for each correct answer (given in italics below). You will need to keep score as you go. The questions to ask are as follows:

Boys' Questions:
1. Mascara is used for:
   a.   Masking the face
   b.   *Darkening the eyelashes*
   c.   Outlining the lips
   d.   Scaring away guys

2. Girls go to the bathroom together because:
   a.   *They can talk about boys*
   b.   They're scared to go alone
   c.   Girls' bathrooms require an escort
   d.   They can do each other's hair

3. What is a "pedicure?"
   a.   A cure for your pet
   b.   A type of makeup
   c.   Getting your hair done
   d.   *Having your toenails painted*

4. What is a "twin set"?
   a.   Buying two blouses for the price of one
   b.   Two girls who choose to dress alike
   c.   *A short-sleeved sweater and long-sleeved sweater*
   d.   A type of pantyhose

5. When might a woman wear a garter?
   a.   When she's mowing the lawn
   b.   *At her wedding*
   c.   While pregnant
   d.   Every other Tuesday

Girls' Questions

1. What is a "fan belt"?
   a. A novelty item sold at sporting events
   b. An electrician's tool
   c. *The belt on the fan that cools the radiator in a car*
   d. A dance move in country western dancing

2. How many outs are there in half an inning?
   a. 3
   b. 6
   c. 9
   d. 12

3. At what age does a man become eligible to be drafted into the military?
   a. 16
   b. 18
   c. 21
   d. 25

4. Why do guys go to the bathroom alone?
   a. They like their privacy
   b. They're embarrassed to ask their friends to go with them
   c. The men's room has limited space (standing room only)
   d. It is a right of passage to prove their manhood

5. What is "WD-40"?
   a. A type of jet
   b. A play in football
   c. *A lubricant used on machinery*
   d. A way to cook your meat (well done for 40 minutes)

Award prizes to the winning team, and then explain that in this game, each side revealed its knowledge or lack of knowledge about the opposite sex. As junior-highers, they are going through many changes. Some of these, as we have already discussed previously, are physical changes. But there are also emotional changes—especially in how they feel about members of the opposite sex. Given this, today the group is going explore how God wants young men and women to treat each other.

MESSAGE

Option 1: Pie Face. For this option you will need several Bibles, several cans of whipped cream, paper plates, two large garbage bags, scissors, two plastic chairs, a plastic drop cloth (to protect the floor) and water and paper towels for clean up. Ahead of time, cut holes in the bottoms of the trash bags, making sure they are big enough for a student's head to fit through. Also set up the tarp and chairs for the game.

Choose two volunteers who are really good friends to play the game, and then direct them to the contest area. Give each volunteer a garbage bag to wear over his or her clothing. Begin preparing seven pies by filling the empty plates with the canned whipped cream. As you do, explain to the volunteers that in this game you are going to ask a series of questions, and the volunteer who raises his or her hand first gets to answer it. If the person answers wrong, his or her opponent gets to "deliver" a pie right in his or her face. If the person answers correctly, he or she will get to deliver the pie to his or her opponent! Here are the trivia questions:

- In what year did the War of 1812 take place? (*1812.*)
- How long did the Hundred Years' War last? (*116 years, from 1337 to 1453.*)
- Who is buried in Grant's Tomb? (*Ulysses S. Grant and his wife.*)
- What is the square root of 81? (*Nine.*)
- How many countries are there in the U.S.? (*One. There are 50 states.*)
- True or False: Noah parted the Red Sea and led his people out of Egypt. (*False. It was Moses.*)
- What date is your best friend's birthday? (*The first person to answer gets to deliver the pie.*)
- Who wants the final pie in the face? (*Whoever raises his or her hand first gets a pie in the face.*)

As the contestants are cleaning up, ask them the following questions:

- Did you want to get a pie in your face? (*Probably not.*)
- Did you want to put a pie in your friend's face? (*Absolutely!*)
- Why did you want to do something to your friend that you didn't want done to you? (*Because it was part of the game.*)

Explain that we often do things to other people that we wouldn't want to have done to us. The same is true in our relationships with members of the opposite sex. Distribute the Bibles and choose one volunteer to read Mark 12:28-31. Explain that in this passage, a teacher of the law came to Jesus with a sincere question. He wanted to know what commandment was the most important to obey.[1]

Jesus answered the man's question by quoting two passages from the Old Testament: Deuteronomy 6:4-5 and Leviticus 19:18. He told the teacher of the law that we are to love God with everything that is in us—our hearts, souls, minds, and all our strength. As we love God, we will be motivated to love other people as we love ourselves. Loving God and loving other people go together.

Conclude by stating that in our pie-throwing exercise, we saw two friends who weren't exactly loving each other as they would want to be loved. Yes, it was just a game, but let's take it one step further and think about how all of our relationships would be different if we loved each other as we want to be loved. This applies to our relationships with the opposite sex as well.

Option 2: Smash the Frame. For this option, you need several Bibles, an adult volunteer, a framed picture of someone dear to you, and a hammer. (Note: you will be smashing the frame, so make sure you copy the picture and put it in a cheap frame. You don't want to take a chance on ruining the original picture!) Ahead of time, arrange a signal to let your adult volunteer know when to smash the picture frame.

Begin by asking the group members to remember those days long ago when hitting someone of the opposite gender was a sign of affection, or when it was considered totally gross to be seen around someone of the opposite sex. Now, as they enter junior high, they are beginning to see things differently. With this change comes a new set of rules for how they are supposed to treat each other. Read John 13:34-35. Explain to the group that God wants us to love each other as Jesus loves us. As we seek to do this, two things will especially help us to love members of the opposite sex in this godly way. The first is to *treat members of the opposite sex as God's special creation.* Have the adult volunteer

Youth Leader Tip

Your group members want to hear stories about the struggles you went through when you were their age. They want to know you can relate to what they are going through now, so be open to sharing your stories.

hold up the picture while you share a little bit about the person who is in it and why he or she means so much to you. Give the signal for the adult volunteer to use the hammer to smash the frame, making sure to *really* damage it.

Explain that this is exactly what we do when we mistreat a member of the opposite sex. God created every single person on earth—and every single person is special to Him. When we make fun of, tease or put down members of the opposite sex, we are hurting God. We ignore the value that God has placed on each person and the love He has for each and every one of us. Remember that Jesus loved us so much that He suffered unimaginable pain on the cross for us.

Continue by stating the second thing that will help us love members of the opposite sex a godly way is *treat them as we want to be treated.* This is actually a command that God gave to His people in the Bible: "Do not seek revenge or bear a grudge against one of your people, but love your neighbor as yourself" (Leviticus 19:18). Teasing and name-calling can be hurtful, and it is certainly not something we would want someone else to do to us. So, in all of our relationships—including those with the opposite sex—we need to change our thinking and love others as Christ loves us.

DIG

Option 1: Acting Out. For this option, you will need several Bibles, one copy of "Acting Out" (found on the next page), scissors and some students who like to ham it up. Ahead of time, copy and cut apart the scenarios on the handout.

Begin by choosing four volunteers (ideally, two guys and two girls). Pair them up (one guy with one girl) and give each pair a scenario from the handout to act out. After the impromptu performance, read the basic scenario to the audience and ask what they think was the difference between the way the characters acted in each scenario. (*The answer, hopefully, would be that one showed kindness and compassion and the other didn't.*)

Distribute the Bibles and choose a volunteer to read Romans 15:7. Ask the students how their reactions to those of the opposite sex might be different if they were to follow what this verse says. (*They would be kinder and more compassionate.*) Next, choose several volunteers to read the following verses: John 13:14, Romans 12:10, Galatians 5:13, Galatians 6:2 and Ephesians 4:32. Discuss the following questions:

- What keeps us from treating others as the Bible says we should? (*No one else around us is doing it, we're afraid we'll look stupid, we're just selfish.*)

acting out

---

scenario one

Samantha has liked Nathan as long as she can remember. Well . . . at least since the fifth grade. But he doesn't seem to pay much attention to her, except when he needs her help in science. Nathan's friend Will, on the other hand, pays a lot of attention to her—way too much. In fact, after school, Will approached Samantha with a flower in his hand.

act it out

Act out the parts of Will and Samantha as realistically as possible, showing how junior-highers who don't have a relationship with Jesus might act. Keep in mind that Samantha doesn't like Will.

---

scenario two

Samantha has liked Nathan as long as she can remember. Well . . . at least since the fifth grade. But he doesn't seem to pay much attention to her, except when he needs her help in science. Nathan's friend Will, on the other hand, pays a lot of attention to her—way too much. In fact, after school, Will approached Samantha with a flower in his hand.

act it out

Act out the parts of Will and Samantha, keeping Paul's words in Romans 15:7 in mind: "Accept one another, then, just as Christ accepted you, in order to bring praise to God."

- What do we gain from treating each other the way God wants us to? (*The joy of obeying Him, lack of guilt, peace from doing the right thing.*)

Close by stating that God expects us to treat each other in a way that honors the other person. This often requires a change in our thinking as we learn to focus more on the needs of others than on ourselves.

Option 2: No Respect. For this option, you will need nothing, nada, zilch. Share the following case study with your group:

Natalie could not get her mind off Peter. Whenever she talked with her friends, she always said something about Peter. In her eyes, he was the most amazing person in the world. If only he would show a tiny bit of interest in her, she would be perfectly happy for the rest of her life.

One afternoon, Peter and his friends were walking down the hallway where Natalie was standing. As they passed by, Peter glanced at her and said, "Hey, Chubs! How ya doin'?" Natalie smiled back at him. She was not sure how to react to him calling her the nickname the boys at school had given her because of her chubby cheeks.

Peter and his friends continued down the hall, where they passed a girl named Lucy. Lucy wasn't necessarily interested in the boys at her school, but she definitely enjoyed it when they showed interest in her. The attention made her feel good. Natalie watched as Peter gave her an interested look. "Whew! Did you see those curves?" he said to his friends. "That girl is *hot!*"

Once you have finished reading the case study, discuss the following questions as a group:

- Each of these students has an unhealthy attitude toward the opposite sex. What is unhealthy about Natalie's attitude toward Peter? (*She is obsessed with him and thinks he can make her life perfect.*)

- Why is this an unhealthy view? (*What she believes is not true. Peter can't make her life perfect, and it's unfair to put that kind of unrealistic expectation on another person.*)

- Peter has a few unhealthy perspectives of his own. What is wrong with the way he acted toward Natalie? (*Even though he was probably just kidding around when he called her "Chubs," it could still hurt her feelings. The fact that Natalie smiled back doesn't mean she was unaffected by the comment, and her apparent acceptance of Peter's remark might make him think it's okay to make jokes about other girls' physical appearances.)*

- What is wrong with the way he acted toward Lucy? *(Peter's attitude toward Lucy is purely physical—he is focused on her body, as if she were an object. If Peter continues to view girls in this manner, he will have a difficult time focusing on the person who is inside the body, and he will have trouble developing meaningful relationships with the opposite sex.)*

- What is unhealthy about Lucy's perspective of guys? *(She doesn't really respect their feelings and is only out to make herself feel good. If she continues to seek appreciation for her looks alone, eventually she'll develop an unhealthy self-image, which will hurt her later in life. She also runs the risk of hurting the boys' feelings with her games.)*

Conclude by stating that Peter, Natalie and Lucy all showed a lack of respect toward the opposite sex by their thoughts and actions, and because of this unhealthy perspective, they hurt not only each other but also themselves. In Matthew 7:12, Jesus says, "Do to others what you would have them do to you." We are to treat others in a way that honors them and communicates our respect to them. This often requires a change in our thinking as we focus more on the needs of others than on ourselves.

APPLY

Option 1: What Happens Next? For this option, you will need several adult volunteers of both sexes, an age-appropriate clip from a television program that shows girls and guys interacting, and a way to show it to your group. In choosing the scene, try to find a two- to five-minute clip that will leave students won-

Youth Leader Tip
Don't be afraid to admit that you've made mistakes—without going into too much detail—and that you hope your group members won't have to suffer the same consequences. Your example can provide a helpful lesson to them.

dering how the characters will act toward each other next. Have the scene ready to show to the group before the session begins.

Show the scene to your group, and then discuss the following questions:

- What are some things the characters did in this scene that are similar to the way the Bible says we should treat the opposite sex?

- How should they act differently in order to treat each other the way the Bible says they should?

Choose several volunteers to play the roles of the characters in the scene. The group members can incorporate ideas from the previous discussion or come up with some new ideas of their own. Ask them to first act out what would happen next if the characters decided to treat each other *differently* than the Bible says they should. Afterward, ask the volunteers to act out what would happen next if the characters were to treat each other in the way the Bible says they should.

Allow time for a couple of different sets of volunteers to come forward and act out the scenes. Close in prayer, thanking God for the opportunities He has given us to see the opposite sex in a more positive way. Ask Him to continue help the group members make good choices in the way they show His love to others.

Option 2: Make It a Reality. For this option, you need several Bibles, a whiteboard and a whiteboard marker.

Begin by distributing the Bibles to the group members, and then choose a volunteer to read 1 John 4:7. Ask what they think would happen if we were to love one another as these verses tell us. (*The answer would be that others would see we are followers of Christ.*) Next, divide the students into two groups by drawing an imaginary line down the middle of the room. Tell the groups that you are going to ask them a series of questions and that you want them to be honest and sincere with their answers. Allow both sides to answer each question, and write their responses on the whiteboard.

- In a youth group where people truly love one another, what kinds of things might the guys do for the girls? (*Some answers might include show good manners, be respectful, don't make rude comments, says positive and encouraging things to one another.*)

- What kinds of things might the girls do for the guys? (*Some answers include show respect, say thank you if a guy holds a door open for them, don't flirt with them just to watch them squirm, be encouraging to them.*)

- Does our youth group do these things for one another? (*You'll need some honest answers here, but don't let anyone talk specifically about someone in the group—in other words, don't use any names.*)
- How do we need to change in the way we treat one another so we can better show God's love to one another? (*Allow group members to answer.*)

Challenge students to make some of the ideas they came up a reality by committing to treat each other with respect and kindness. Invite them to come forward and place their initials on the whiteboard next to the idea or ideas they are willing to start doing this week. Close in prayer, thanking God for the opportunity the group has to continue to treat one another with Christ's love. Ask God to give the students the boldness to carry out any changes they feel they need to make.

REFLECT

The following short devotions are for the group members to reflect on and answer during the week. You can make a copy of these pages and distribute to your class or download and print from **www.gospellight.com/uncommon/jh_dealing_with_pressure.zip**.

1—A SEASON FOR EVERYTHING

What time is it? Look up Ecclesiastes 3:1.

This is no denying it: things change. Sometimes you will welcome the change, such as when your parents give you more responsibility or let you do things they didn't used to allow you to do. Sometimes the change will not be as welcome, such as when your parents begin to require more from you because you are older, or your feelings toward members of the opposite sex begins to change!

What does Ecclesiastes 3:1 say about change?

- ☐ It happens, and we should worry about it.
- ☐ It happens, so there is no need to make any plans for the future.
- ☐ It happens, but always in God's timing.
- ☐ It happens, so we should always put a big smile on our faces and be completely happy about it.

What is one change you are facing today that has you concerned?

_____

_____

_____

_____

_____

How can you give that concern to God?

_____

_____

_____

_____

_____

Change happens, but always in God's timing. So remember today that no matter what you are facing, God will always be there to see you through. Thank Him today that He will help you through every situation in your life and that He will never leave you.

2—BE KIND TO OTHERS

Check out Ephesians 4:32 for a little lesson in kindness.

Troy liked to tease the girls in his class. His specialty was pointing out certain things about them that he knew they were self-conscious about—their hair, or their clothes, or some little quirk they had. He thought it was all good fun, and the girls all seemed to take it well . . . or so he thought.

Imagine Troy's surprise one day when his friend Mike told him that he had seen a girl he had teased in tears. The girl had laughed when Troy had made the comment, so he couldn't understand why she would have gotten so upset. Troy asked Mike if maybe something else had upset her, but Mike said that he had overheard the girl talking about the rude comment Troy had made to her.

If you were Troy, what would you do at this point?

_____

_____

_____

_____

Why is it important to be kind to others in your school?

_____

_____

_____

_____

Why is it important to show respect when dealing with members of the op-posite sex?

_____

_____

_____

_____

At times, all of us have made a comment that we later regretted making. This is why it is so important to practice respect. Today, ask God to help you grow in this area so that you can be kind and respectful in your conversations.

3—KEEP CALAMITY AWAY

What does gossip bring? Read Proverbs 21:23 to find out.

It can be *soooo* tempting to spread rumors about who likes who among your circle of friends. After all, everybody does it, and you don't want to be left out of the fun—or seem strange for not taking part. Who doesn't like a good bit of gossip? It seems like just a harmless bit of good fun.

What does Proverbs 21:23 say about this?

_____

_____

_____

"Calamity" can be defined as "a disaster that causes suffering." How can spreading rumors and lies about another person cause calamity, even if you didn't intend any harm?

_____

_____

_____

_____

God wants you to use words to build others up, not tear them down. A good way to do this is by not taking part in gossiping about others. Once again, this will likely require a change in your thinking and a commitment to not to go along with the crowd when your friends start saying things about another person. So ask God for the strength—and keep the calamity away!

4—WHEN *NOT* TO REJOICE

Don't gloat! Turn to Proverbs 24:17-18.

Edward had a crush on Bella, the new girl at school. The only problem was that Jacob, one of the most popular boys in his class, also seemed to have feelings for her. Edward thought Bella would never be interested in him, but much to his surprise, she started smiling at him and finding excuses to come up and talk to him in the hall.

Of course, Edward wanted to drop some not-so-subtle hits to Jacob that he wasn't as great as he thought he was. But then he remembered that Proverbs 24:17-18 tells us to . . .

❑   Not gloat, unless the person is really asking for it.
❑   Not gloat, though we can be a bit happy about it.
❑   Not gloat, but tell our friends all about it.
❑   Not gloat, because this doesn't please God.

In what ways can your feelings about a person of the opposite sex have a negative impact on your relationships with your friends?

_____
_____
_____
_____

Why it is important to never gloat with your friends when someone of the opposite sex is interested in you?

_____
_____
_____
_____
_____

What should you do when you find yourself in a situation like Edward's?

_____

_____

_____

_____

Today, ask God to give you wisdom in all of your relationships—both with your friends and with those of the opposite sex.

CHANGES IN OUR BODIES

THE BIG IDEA

As our bodies change and mature, we need to remember that God created them and sees them as being a holy place where He dwells.

SESSION AIMS

In this session, you will guide group members to (1) recognize that their physical bodies are changing; (2) understand that God wants them to avoid sexual sin and to honor Him with their bodies; and (3) commit to remaining sexually pure and allowing God to work through them during this time in their lives.

THE BIGGEST VERSE

"Flee from sexual immorality. All other sins a man commits are outside his body, but he who sins sexually sins against his own body" (1 Corinthians 6:18).

OTHER IMPORTANT VERSES

Genesis 1:26-27; Psalm 139:14; 1 Corinthians 6:19-20; 15:51-54; Galatians 1:10; 1 Thessalonians 4:3

Note: Additional options and worksheets in 8$^1/_2$" x 11" format for this session are available for download at **www.gospellight.com/uncommon/jh_dealing_with_pressure.zip**.

STARTER

Option 1: The Makeover. For this session, you need scissors, two jumbo-sized trash bags, two sets of makeup products (lipstick, eyeliner and so forth), and facial wipes for cleanup. Ahead of time, use the scissors to cut a hole in the bottom of the trash bags, making sure it is big enough to fit over a student's head.

Greet the students and choose two guy volunteers and four girl volunteers. Divide the volunteers into two teams—one guy and two girls in each. Give one trash bag to each of the two guys to wear (these will serve as "styling aprons"). Once the guys are ready for their makeovers, give each team a set of makeup. Let the girls on the teams know that they have two minutes to do a complete makeover on the boy in their group. Give the signal for the teams to begin. Ask the teams to stop when two minutes are up, and have the audience vote by applauding for the best makeover.

After you are finished with the fun (and while the guys are wiping off all the goop), explain that people get makeovers to change their appearance. Some people might not like a certain physical attribute, and so they will use a makeover to hide attributes or make them less obvious. On the other hand, some people might like a certain part of their appearance, so they will use a makeover to emphasize it.

Continue by stating that no matter how old a person is, his or her body is always physically changing. Ask the group members to list some ways they think junior-highers bodies might be changing at this time. (*Some answers might include they are getting bigger, their voices are changing, their body hair is beginning to grow, their muscles are developing, and so on.*) Explain that God is responsible for all of these changes.

Conclude by stating that sometimes it's easy to forget that we are God's creation and that He designed us exactly the way He wants us to be. Just because we're growing and changing doesn't make that fact less true. Today, as we start this new series on changes, we're going to look at how we need to honor our God with the bodies He has given us—including honoring Him with the choices we make concerning our sexuality.

Option 2: Clothes Relay. For this option, you will need an adult volunteer, a washable felt-tip marker, and two sets of clothing (a large pair of sweat pants, a large shirt, tie, hat, shoes and so on) for a relay race.

Greet the group members and divide them into two teams (or more if the group is larger than 20 students). Designate one team as "Team #1" and the other as "Team #2." Use the felt-tip pen to write a "1" on the hands of all Team

#1 members and a "2" on the hands of all Team #2 members (and so on for any additional teams).

Divide each team in half. Have one half go to the right side of the room and the other half go to the left side of the room. Give a set of clothes to the members from Teams #1 and #2 who are on the right side of the room. When you give the signal, the first person on each team will need to put on all of the clothes, run to the other side of the room (where the other half of his or her team is), and take off the clothes he or she has just put on. Now the first person in line on the left side of the room will put on all of the clothes and repeat the process. Continue until each person on a team has put on and taken off the clothes one time. The first team to get through all of its players and sit down is the winner.

When the game is finished, explain that they might feel as if they are physically changing almost as often as they changed their clothes in the game today. Ask them to list some ways that their bodies are changing during this time in their life. (*Some answers might include that they are getting taller, their voices are changing, they have more body hair, their muscles are developing, and so on.*)

Explain that God is responsible for these changes, and He designed us exactly the way He wants us to be. Today as we start this new series on change, we are going to look at how we need to honor God with the bodies He has given us. That includes honoring Him with the choices we make concerning our sexuality.

MESSAGE

Option 1: People Structures. For this option, you will need several Bibles and prizes. Begin by dividing the group members into team of 6 to 10 people. Explain that you will be naming some famous structures. After you read each one, the members from each team must work together to form a human version of that structure. Each one will be judged, and the winning team will be awarded 10,000 points for that round. Begin the game by naming the following buildings (feel free to add more from your own town!):

- St. Louis Arch
- Golden Gate Bridge
- Egyptian Pyramids
- Leaning Tower of Pisa
- Eiffel Tower
- Washington Monument

When the game is finished and all of points have been added up, award prizes to the winning team. Transition to the message by that stating that each of our bodies are structures as well. Distribute the Bibles and ask a volunteer to read 1 Corinthians 6:18-20 to the group.[1] When the volunteer has read the verses, explain that some people—even some Christians—think they have the right to do whatever they want with their bodies. But the truth is that our bodies—including our minds—belong to God.

This passage gives us two reasons why we should avoid sexual sin: (1) because our bodies are temples of the Holy Spirit (see verse 19), and (2) because we were "bought at a price" (verse 20). Just like a building, our bodies are the house of God, and they need to be a sacred place where the Holy Spirit can work within us. In addition, God sent His Son, Jesus, to be our sacrifice and the ultimate payment for our sin. When we accept Jesus' payment, we are considered to be bought by God. Our bodies are to be used to honor Him.

Conclude by stating that God is not a big stick-in-the-mud out to ruin our fun. As we will see next, He knows what is best for us, and He wants to protect us from some really bad stuff that happens when we use our changing bodies the wrong way.

Option 2: Bought at a Price. For this option, you will need a jar with a lid, a votive candle, some wooden fireplace or barbecue matches, a checkbook and a couple of bills.

Begin by stating that with the changes that are taking place in the group members' lives right now come new temptations—especially sexual ones. In the Bible, we find a group of people who were struggling mightily with these kinds of sexual temptations: the believers in the Corinthian church. They were committing sexual sins, so Paul needed to set them straight.

Read 1 Corinthians 6:18-20 and explain that these verses give us two reasons why we should avoid sexual sins and honor God with our bodies. The first reason is found in verse 19: "Your body is a temple of the Holy Spirit." Hold up

Youth Leader Tip

To get maximum participation from students during discussion times, have them first share ideas with partners or small groups. The smaller the setting, the safer the group members will feel in sharing their thoughts.

the jar. State that when we become Christians, God gives us His Holy Spirit, who actually comes to dwell within us. Place the candle in the jar. State that when this happens, we become a home to God. Light the candle. Explain that when the Holy Spirit is working in us, He transforms us and enables us to reflect God's glory to others.

State that our bodies need to be places where the Holy Spirit can work. However, sometimes we do things with our bodies—such as entertaining sexual thoughts—that don't honor God. Place the lid on the jar and extinguish the flame of the candle. Explain that when we act as if we're in control instead of God, we prevent His Holy Spirit from shining through our lives. We need to recognize that the Holy Spirit is in us. Because of this, we need to keep our bodies as places that honor Him.

Continue by stating that the second reason why we need to avoid sexual sin is found in verse 20: "You were bought at a price." In the Old Testament, when people needed to be forgiven of their sins, they had to sacrifice an animal to God. This animal had to be perfect, with no blemishes. The blood of the animal covered (or "atoned") for the sin of the people. The reason it was called a sacrifice is because the people had to give up something valuable to pay for their sins.

Hold up the checkbook. State that every month their parents have to pay bills, and some bills require a higher payment than others. In the same way, humankind's sin required a costly payment. Write a check for $1 million and pass it around. State that even this check for $1 million would not make up for our sin. There is no amount of payment that we could make—no matter how high— that would free us from our sins. That payment had to come from God Himself.

Conclude by stating that because of God's great love for us, He agreed to make this final payment for us. He sent His Son, Jesus, to serve as the ultimate sacrifice and the final payment for our sin. God bought us with this payment, and so, when we accept Jesus Christ as our Savior, He considers us to be His. We are in His service, which is why we need to honor Him with our bodies.

DIG

Option 1: Examine the Consequences. For this option, you will need the movie *10 Things I Hate About You* and a way to show it to your group. Ahead of time, find the scene in which the father asks, "Do you know anything about this party?" followed by the scene where he has his daughter put on a fake pregnancy pillow to remind her of the consequences of sexual sin. Have the scene ready to show to your group before the session begins. (Note: this movie is rated PG-13 for references to sexuality, language and references to drinking and drug use, so be sure to just show the selected scene.)

Once you have shown the movie clip, discuss the following questions:

- Why did the girl's dad want her to wear the pregnancy outfit? (*He wanted her to realize one of the possible consequences of having sex.*)

- What are some of the negative outcomes of sex before marriage? (*AIDS/HIV, unwanted pregnancy, sexually transmitted diseases, broken relationships, hurt feelings and shame, among many others.*)

- What are some reasons people decide to have sex before they get married? (*Because they are curious, it feels good, they are lonely, it's considered the "next step" in a relationship, because of peer pressure, and so on.*)

Explain that at this time in the group member's lives, the onset of puberty and the hormones that come with it can cause them to think about sexuality more than they ever have before. This is a signal that God is preparing their bodies for adulthood and a sexual relationship when they get married. Yep, God created sex. He gave us sex as an intimate expression of our love for one another *when we are married.*

Ask the group members to think about how they might deal with the temptation to have sex before they are married. Allow a few volunteers to give their answers. Continue by explaining that it is important for them to make some decisions about how they are going to respond to the temptation and pressure of sex *before* they are faced with it—because they *will* definitely face it.

Option 2: Steve and Sherri. For this option, you will need a whiteboard and a whiteboard marker. Begin by asking a male student to read aloud the following case study:

Steve had two great loves: God and surfing. One day while he was out catches some waves, he met an awesome girl named Sherri. Steve had never met anyone who seemed so perfect for him. As the weeks went by, Steve liked Sherri more and more—she was easy to talk to, and he always had fun when they were together. After dating for a couple of months, the other surfers wanted to know how far Steve and Sherri had gone. Steve was embarrassed to say that they had barely even kissed. Feeling the pressure, he decided that he and Sherri needed to take their relationship to the next level. So, that night, he began pressuring Sherri to have sex with him.

Now ask a female student to read Sherri's side of the story:

Sherri loved the beach and was a faithful member of her church's youth group. One day while she was relaxing at the beach with friends, she noticed a good-looking surfer. On a dare, she paddled out to where he was waiting to catch a wave to see if she could meet him. The surfer's name was Steve, and they immediately hit it off. As the weeks went by, the thing Sherri liked most about Steve was that he didn't try to impress her. He was just himself. She loved being with him because he made her feel good about who she was. Then, a couple of months into their relationship, something changed. Steve began pressuring her into being more intimate. She tried to resist the pressure, but she worried that she might lose Steve if she didn't give in. Finally, she did.

Now discuss the following questions:

- What are some of negative ways this story could end? (*Sherri could get pregnant, she could get an STD, they could break up.*)

- Why did Steve make the decision to pressure Sherri into having sex? (*He felt pressure from his peer group—the other surfers—and realized that he might not be cool or fit in if he didn't have sex.*)

- Why did Sherri make the decision to have pre-marital sex? (*She was afraid Steve would leave her if she didn't give in.*)

- What are some other reasons people decide to have sex before they get married? (*Because they are curious, it feels good, they are lonely, it's considered the "next step" in a relationship, in response to peer pressure.*)

Continue by stating that sex in itself is not bad—in fact, *God created it.* However, He has always intended sex to only be between people who are in a marriage relationship. This can be difficult for teens, because when the hormones begin to kick in at the onset of puberty, the sexual urges begin to rise. These changes in their bodies are an indication that God is preparing them for adulthood and a sexual relationship when they get married, but it can be difficult to wait—especially when it seems that everyone else around is "doing it."

But we must remember that God gave us sex as an intimate expression of our love for one another *when we are married.*

Now discuss the following questions as a group:

- What are some of the consequences of sex outside of marriage? (*AIDS/ HIV, unwanted pregnancy, sexually transmitted diseases, broken relationships, hurt feelings and shame, among many others.*)

- Why do you think God wants sex only to be shared between a man and a woman who are married? (*To protect us from harm. The negative consequences of sex outside of marriage are generally eliminated when it we use sex as God intended—for two people joined in marriage.*)

- What are some ways that Steve and Sherri could have avoided making the mistake they did? (*They could have avoided this mistake by sticking to their convictions and communicating with each other. It would also have helped if they had made a commitment not to have sex before they got into this situation.*)

Explain that just like Steve and Sherri, we will be faced with temptations to have sex before marriage. These temptations are not going to disappear. For this reason, we need to develop a solid plan for how to handle those situations right now.

APPLY

Option 1: Just a Little. For this option, you will need three volunteers, three copies of "Just a Little" (found on the next page), a cup of dirt, bottled water (one for every student), and one clear glass filled with water. Ahead of time, give copies of the skit to the volunteers and ask them to practice their assigned roles. (Note: Friend 1 is a girl and Friends 2 and 3 are both guys, but you can reverse the roles if you want to do so.) Make sure that any prop used in the skit is ready to go.

Ask the volunteers to perform the skit (you will be the narrator), and then explain that there is an important truth in this little play that they shouldn't miss. The water represents their bodies—clean and pure—the way God made them. God expects them to honor Him by keeping their changing bodies pure for Him and for their future spouses. However, in order to stay sexually pure, they will need to make the decision *right now* to resist the temptation to give their purity to someone before marriage.

Just a Little

Characters	**Props**
Friend 1 (a girl)	A clear glass filled
Friend 2 (a guy)	with water
Friend 3 (a guy)	A cup of dirt

The scene opens with Friend 1 enjoying an ice-cold glass of water. Friend 2 approaches.

Friend 2:   Hey! What's up? WOW! That looks like a great glass of water! Mind if I take a sip?

Friend 1:   Well, I've already promised to share it with someone else.

Friend 2:   It really looks good. I'm so thirsty! *We're* friends too, aren't we?

Friend 1:   (*Hesitates.*) Well, yeah, we're friends (*Pauses.*) But I promised I would only share it with him.

Friend 2:   C'mon, he won't even know.

Friend 1:   I guess you're right. Just a little sip, though, okay?

Friend 2:   (*Getting excited.*) Yeah, okay. Just a little sip. (*He reaches for glass and turns to face the audience as he takes a sip. He reaches into the cup of dirt and adds a handful to the water. He turns back around and hands the glass to Friend 1.*) Thanks! I really enjoyed that! Well, see ya! (*Walks off.*)

Friend 1 is left holding the dirty water, looking at it with a sad expression. Just then Friend 3 approaches, whistling.

Friend 3:   Hey! How are you? Do you have the water you promised . . . (*Stops suddenly and points to the water.*) Is *that* the water you brought to share with me?

Distribute the bottled water and invite the group members to take a look at the water in the bottles before opening them. Point out how clear and pure it is, and then explain that if they are sexually pure right now, they need to ask God to help them remain that way in the midst of changing hormones and new temptations. If they have already made some sexual mistakes, then they can ask God to give them the strength they need to remain pure from now on.

Allow a moment of silent prayer time for the group members to ask God to help them in their quest to remain sexually pure, even as their hormones are racing faster and faster. When this is completed, lead the group in a closing prayer, thanking God for the gifts He has given them and asking Him to help them stay sexually pure until marriage. Ask for His will to be done in all areas of their lives and for the Holy Spirit to empower them to stand strong in the face of temptation.

Option 2: Sexual Purity Cards. For this option, you will need an adult volunteer, copies of "Sexual Purity Cards" (found on the next page) and some extra-virgin olive oil (available at your local grocery store). Ahead of time, copy the handout and cut them into individual cards.

Begin by stating that in the Old Testament, a ceremony was held whenever someone or something was dedicated to God. During this ceremony, the priest would put holy oil on the person or thing, thus "anointing" it and declaring that it now belonged to God. That person or thing was now set apart for His sacred use. The Israelites didn't make these commitments to God lightly—and neither should we. So, when we make a commitment to God to do something—such as keeping our bodies pure for the person we will marry—it represents a promise from us to God.

Explain that you have mentioned this because you are going to be passing out some cards in which they will be given the opportunity to make a similar type of commitment to God. These cards represent a way that they can make a *conscious* decision to not have sex *before* they get into a situation where they feel pressured to do so. Point out that if they have already made some mistakes in this area, it's not too late. They can make a new commitment, and they can choose to remain pure before God from that moment on.

Allow some time for silent prayer, encouraging the group members to ask God if now is the time for them to make this commitment to sexual purity. After a few minutes, distribute the "Sexual Purity Cards" and pens or pencils. Invite those who are willing to make the commitment to sign the cards and then come forward so you can anoint them with oil, declaring that they belong to

SEXUAL PURITY CARDS

I, _____, being a child of God and set apart for His use, commit to a life of sexual purity. I commit to honoring God with my body and mind. I will pray daily for the strength to follow Him.

I, _____, being a child of God and set apart for His use, commit to a life of sexual purity. I commit to honoring God with my body and mind. I will pray daily for the strength to follow Him.

I, _____, being a child of God and set apart for His use, commit to a life of sexual purity. I commit to honoring God with my body and mind. I will pray daily for the strength to follow Him.

I, _____, being a child of God and set apart for His use, commit to a life of sexual purity. I commit to honoring God with my body and mind. I will pray daily for the strength to follow Him.

God. Ask them to keep the cards handy to serve as a reminder of their commitment to remain pure.

Invite those you anointed (and other last-minute decision makers) to stay after the meeting so you and the adult volunteer can meet and pray with them. Close the general group session time together in prayer, thanking God for all the gifts He has given—including the gift of a sexual relationship within marriage. Ask Him to help everyone in the group to stay sexually pure in the face of pressure to conform.

REFLECT

The following short devotions are for the group members to reflect on and answer during the week. You can make a copy of these pages and distribute to your class or download and print from **www.gospellight.com/uncommon/jh_dealing_with_pressure.zip.**

1—WONDERFULLY MADE

If you *wonder* how you are made, read Psalm 139:14.

Imagine you wake up one morning with three huge zits on your nose and chin. You have a wicked case of bed hair, and the only clean clothes you can find are the ones in the back of your closet that don't look good on you.

As you arrive at school, you're sure that *everyone* is looking at your zits. Just as you sink into your chair, the principal's voice comes over the intercom with the morning announcements—including the reminder that you'll be presenting the results of your research project in front of the *entire* school this afternoon.

Your friend, a photographer for the school yearbook committee and the newspaper, says, "This is *so* great! Your picture's gonna be in the yearbook and the school newspaper! *And* the local TV news is going to be here to cover the story!" What do you do?

- ❏ Pretend you're sick and call your mom to pick you up early.
- ❏ Ask your friends to switch clothes with you, loan you a hat, or even pretend to be you.
- ❏ Say you left your project at home and ask if you can do it another day.
- ❏ Follow through on your commitment, trusting that other people won't notice your faults.

We all have *something* we'd like to change about our appearance. What are some things about your appearance that bother you?

_____

_____

_____

_____

According to Psalm 139:14, how do you think God sees you?

_____

_____

_____

_____

How do you think He wants you to see yourself and others?

_____

_____

_____

_____

Even though some days you feel like a reject, it just isn't true. Each of us is an amazing creation that God has made. So, the next time you feel unattractive, remind yourself that you are wonderfully and purposefully made by God Himself!

2—ALL THIS CHANGE!

In whose image are you made? Read Genesis 1:26-27 to find out.

Trevor was confused by all the changes taking place in his body. He grew three inches in one summer and none of his clothes fit anymore, his voice changed, people started calling him "young man," and to top it all off he started thinking about girls in a way that he hadn't before. It was all so weird and embarrassing.

During Sunday school one week, Trevor's teacher talked about God's creation. "All during the creation, God noticed that what He was creating was good," the Sunday school teacher said. "But after the sixth day, when God had made humans, He noticed that what He had created was *very good*. You are God's masterpiece—the final piece of artwork that God put together with some of His own characteristics."

Trevor hadn't thought about it that way before. He didn't need to be embarrassed by the changes in his body. After all, everyone has to go through them. It's all a part of the wonder of God's creation!

How do you feel about your changing body?

_____
_____
_____
_____

What do you think would happen if your body didn't change like the other kids?

_____
_____
_____
_____

Today, think of three things you like about yourself, and then thank God for them.

3—KNOCK IT OFF!

Who are you trying to please? Read Galatians 1:10 to find out Paul's answer.

Imagine you're sitting in study hall when someone passes you a note. You read it and realize that one of the most attractive and popular kids in the school has sent it to you. The note, however, makes inappropriate mention of the private parts of your body. What do you do?

- ☐ Crumple the note and throw it at the person who sent it.
- ☐ Pass a note back, making some comment about that particular person's private parts.
- ☐ Ask the person not to send notes or say these inappropriate things to you. In other words, "Knock it off!"

When you hear these discussions at school, should you get involved in them? Why or why not?

_____
_____
_____
_____

What do you think God would say if He joined the discussion?

_____

_____

_____

_____

According to Galatians 1:10, are we supposed to go along with what every-one else is doing? Why or why not?

_____

_____

_____

_____

Today, ask God to help you keep your mind on Him and what He has for you—even when those around you want you to join in with what they are doing.

4—TAKE HOPE

Take hope and read 1 Corinthians 15:51-54.

When Gina's grandpa died, everyone kept saying, "It's for the best. He was in so much pain." Gina knew that was true. Her grandpa's body had been de-teriorating for years. He had had a bad heart, sore joints and brittle bones, and he couldn't see well or hear most of what Gina said to him. In fact, he had said he was looking forward to "going home" to be with Jesus.

At her grandpa's funeral, Gina heard the pastor read from 1 Corinthians 15:51-54. He said, "Let's find hope in this passage. In heaven, there is no fear, no crying and no pain. Death itself has been swallowed up in victory!" Gina still missed her grandpa terribly, but whenever she felt sad, she reminded herself that her grandpa was in heaven with a brand new body, enjoying the company of Jesus Himself!

The wonderful bodies that God has given us will one day break down, get sick and die. It will happen to each of us, no matter who we are. But what does this passage promise to those who belong to God?

_____

_____

_____

_____

What does it mean to you when you read that "death has been swallowed up in victory"?

_____

_____

_____

_____

The bodies we have now are only temporary. But for those who follow Jesus, death is not the end. So thank God today for the body that He has given you, and praise Him for the promise He has made that you will one day spend eternity with Him.

CHANGES IN OUR RELATIONSHIP WITH GOD

THE BIG IDEA

Our God never changes, but as we grow closer to Him, our relationship with Him does.

SESSION AIMS

In this session, you will guide group members to (1) understand that God wants their relationships with Him to continue changing and growing; (2) be motivated to let God change their hearts and actions; and (3) choose to make changes in their life that will allow their relationships with God to develop.

THE BIGGEST VERSE

"But God demonstrates his own love for us in this: While we were still sinners, Christ died for us" (Romans 5:8).

OTHER IMPORTANT VERSES

Psalm 18:2; John 15:14-15; Romans 5:6-11; James 1:17; 1 John 1:5,9-10

Note: Additional options and worksheets in 8¹/₂" x 11" format for this session are available for download at **www.gospellight.com/uncommon/jh_dealing_with_pressure.zip**.

STARTER

Option 1: Characteristics Spud. For this option, you will need a large rubber four-square ball and lots of room.

Welcome the group members and tell them that you are going to be playing a game called "Characteristics Spud."[1] In this game, they will be tossing a rubber ball into the air and quickly calling out another student's name and one thing that is unique about that person. For example, they might call out his or her favorite car, the color of his or her shirt, and so on. The person whose name is called is "It", and he or she must run forward and catch the ball. Meanwhile, the other players will run as far away from It as they can before he or she can catch the ball and call out "Spud!"

At that point, everyone must freeze. The person who is It can take three steps in any direction to get as close as possible to a player in order to hit him or her with the ball. If It is successful, that player becomes It. The process continues, with the next It calling out another student's name and one unique characteristic about him or her. Play the game for as long as you would like, and then discuss the following questions:

- Which of the characteristics you called out had something to do with how the person looked?
- Which of the characteristics had something to do with what was inside that person or with who that person was?
- When you're looking for a friend, what kinds of characteristics or special qualities are important to you?
- How many of you want a friend who will always be there for you and will not fail you? Raise your hands. (*Check the pulse of anyone not raising his or her hand.*)
- How many of you have a friend who is always, *always* there for you?

Explain to the group that no human can always be there for us. Our friends are bound to let us down. However, as we will see today, even as our earthly friends fail us, there is one friend who won't let us down: God.

Option 2: Three-legged Challenge. For this option, you will need a piece of rubber tubing from an inner tube, prizes and several adult volunteers to referee. (Note that rope or string can also be used, but rubber tubing works best because it stretches and bends in case a student falls). Ahead of time, cut the inner tube into sections that are long enough to tie students' legs together for a three-legged race.

Divide the group members into teams of eight people each. Choose four students from each team to go to the opposite side of the room. Distribute the rubber tubing and instruct teammates from both sides to pair up and tie their legs together for a three-legged race. At your signal, one set of teammates from each team will run to the other side of the room and tag the next set of teammates. The tagged teammates will then run to the opposite side of the room, tagging the next set of teammates, and so on. As the teammates cross the room, you will randomly call out different commands (such as "the shorter person of the pair must walk backward," or, "the one who has the biggest thumb must crawl on all fours"). Each time you call out something, the teammates must follow the command until you call out another.

Allow five minutes for the different teams to cross the room as many times as they can. Have someone keep track of each team's crossings. When you are ready to end the game, give the signal for the group members to stop, and then award prizes to the team that successfully crossed the room the most times. Discuss the following questions:

- What were some things that helped you in this race? (*Counting together, coordinating our steps, and so on.*)
- Was communication important during the race? (*Yes.*)
- Would having a close friend to be your partner have helped you in the race? (*Yes. Good friends understand each other and work well together.*)
- Which of the commands were the hardest to obey? Why? (*Allow group members to respond.*)
- Why was this race different than a typical three-legged race? (*The partners were constantly changing the way they were racing.*)

Explain that it can be really hard when the people we're around keep changing. Sometimes the friends we thought would always be there let us down. But today we're going to learn about a friend who never lets us down. No matter how much we change, He never does. His name is God.

Youth Leader Tip

It is important to give your group members regular opportunities to respond to an invitation to know Jesus (or recommit to Him). You might be surprised at who responds and is ready to follow Jesus in a whole new way.

MESSAGE

Option 1: Trick Questions. For this option, you will need several Bibles and this book. Explain that you are going to read a statement. If the group members believe the statement is correct, they need to move to the right side of the room. If they believe the statement is incorrect, they need to move to the left side of the room. Here are the statements:

- There is a fourth of July in England. (*Correct. July 4th happens everywhere.*)
- Only one month has 28 days. (*Incorrect. Every month has 28 days.*)
- A person cannot go eight days without sleep. (*Incorrect. The person can sleep at night.*)
- It is against the law for a man living in North Carolina to be buried in South Carolina. (*Correct. If the man is living, he is not dead yet.*)
- A ton of feathers weighs the same as a ton of bricks. (Correct. *A ton, or 2,000 pounds, is a ton no matter the substance of which it is made.*)

Explain that sometimes it can be difficult in life to figure out the correct answer. It's also tough to know whether or not we are doing right. Distribute the Bibles and choose a volunteer or two to read Romans 5:6-11.[2] After the volunteers have read the passage, discuss the following as a group:

- What is it the Bible says we have done that keeps us from having a friendship with Jesus? (*We have sinned.*)
- Did God just decide it wasn't worth having a relationship with us? (*No.*)
- How did He make a way for us back to Him? (*He sent His Son, Jesus, to die as the payment for our sin.*)

Close by stating that we have all sinned, or "wronged God." Accepting Jesus as our Lord and Savior is the way God has provided to right those wrongs. Read Romans 5:6 aloud again, and explain that friendship with God is a two-way relationship. It means that both God and us must participate. In order for our relationship with God to grow, we need to spend time with Him each day. As we do, we will find that our lives will totally begin to change!

Option 2: Flipping the Magnets. For this option, you will need several Bibles and at least two large magnets.

Choose a volunteer to read Romans 5:6-11. Explain that these verses make it clear that God wants to have a friendship with each of us. We all can know God and have a friendship with him by understanding the three *Rs* from this passage. The first *R* stands for *wrong*. (Okay, technically that word starts with a *W*, but it sounds like an *R*.) The Bible tells us that God is perfect, and "in him there is no darkness at all" (1 John 1:5). However, we are wrong and are full of sin, which prevents us from having a relationship with the Lord. Hold up the magnets and demonstrate how, when they are turned the wrong way, they push away from each other. Continue by stating that this is what happens when we sin—it pushes us away from His presence.

Next, explain that the second *R* stands for *right*. God wants to have a friendship with us, but first He has to make us right. To do this, He sent His Son, Jesus, to die as a payment for our sin. He didn't wait for us to deserve His friendship—He pursued us because He loves us. Jesus' death allows us to be forgiven for everything we have ever done or will ever do against God. If we accept His payment and ask Him to be in charge of our life, we will become right before God. Hold up the magnets and turn them the correct way so they pull each other together. Continue by stating that when we receive forgiveness for our sins, we are made right with God and are drawn into a relationship with Him.

Now explain that the third *R* stands for *relationship*. Because we have been forgiven, we can have a relationship with God. God not only wants to be our friend, but He also wants our friendship in return. Just as we spend time with our friends—talking all the time, looking out for one another, standing up for one another—God wants us to make the effort to show Him our love with our words and actions. We need to talk with Him about our lives. He wants us to tell Him what we are thinking and feeling. Otherwise (pull the magnets apart), we can be pulled away from our relationship with Him. The cool thing is that being friends with God is more than just a chance to hang with Him. A relationship with God will totally change us!

DIG

Option 1: The Doctor's Office. For this option, you will need copies "The Doctor's Office" (found on the next page) and some volunteer actors. Ahead of time, assign each volunteer a part in the skit. Also give the volunteers copies of the play so they can practice their parts.

Introduce the skit, and let the show begin. After the performance is over and the thunderous applause has died down, ask the group members what they think was happening to the first patient who came to the doctor's office for a checkup. (*He caught the illnesses that everyone else had.*) Explain that friendships can be similar. When we spend time with people, we often pick up

THE DOCTOR'S OFFICE

CAST
Patient One, a very healthy guy
Patient Two, an allergy sufferer
Patient Three, a guy suffering
   from an itch
Patient Four, a lady having spasms
Patient Five, a pregnant woman
Receptionist

PROPS
Two chairs, placed side by side
   and facing the audience
Receptionist's desk (a table and
   chair) facing the audience
A pillow (for Patient Five's
   tummy)

The scene opens with a receptionist sitting at a table facing the audience. Patient One enters and goes to the receptionist's desk.

PATIENT ONE: Hello, I'm here to see the doctor for a routine checkup. As you can see, I am the picture of perfect health. (*Flexes muscles.*)

RECEPTIONIST: Very well. The doctor will be with you in a moment. Please take a seat.

(*Patient One sits down.*)

PATIENT TWO: (*Enters, sneezing loudly and uncontrollably.*) I must see the doctor quickly! I've developed some allergy and I'm going crazy. I gotta see the doc!

RECEPTIONIST: There is someone ahead of you, but the doctor will be with you shortly. Please have a seat.

Patient Two sits next to Patient One. Patient One begins to "catch" the illness and starts sneezing—slowly at first, but then as badly as Patient Two. Meanwhile, Patient Two's sneezing decreases until it stops altogether.

PATIENT TWO: (*Stands up.*) You can cancel my appointment. My sneezing has stopped. (*Patient Two leaves.*)

PATIENT THREE: (*Enters, scratching all over.*) Please, I've got to see the doc for this itch. It's driving me insane!

RECEPTIONIST: Please have a seat. The doctor will be right out.

Patient Three sits next to the sneezing Patient One. After a few seconds, the itching has transferred to Patient One, who is now sneezing and itching uncontrollably. Patient Three's itching suddenly stops.

PATIENT THREE: (*Stands up.*) You know what? I feel fine. You can cancel my appointment. (*Patient Three leaves.*)

PATIENT FOUR: (*Enters with a muscle-jerking, arm-flying kick.*) I've got to see the doctor (*Kick!*) immediately. I don't know what's wrong with me! (*Kick!*)

RECEPTIONIST: Yes, please have a seat. The doctor will be with you shortly.

Patient Four sits next to Patient One. Soon Patient One is sneezing, itching and jerking uncontrollably. Patient Four becomes calm, and his jerking stops.

PATIENT FOUR: (*Stands up.*) Hey, I'm feeling better now. You can cancel my appointment. (*Patient Four Leaves.*)

Patient Five, who is obviously pregnant, enters the room.

PATIENT FIVE: (*Staggers in and sits down heavily next to Patient One.*)

PATIENT ONE: (*Stands up screams.*) Oh, no. Not me!

Patient One runs off the stage.

their characteristics, or become like them. Choose a volunteer to share about a time in his or her life when this occurred (such as a time when the person's friends began to use the same slang words, finish each others' sentences, dress the same way, and so on). Now discuss the following questions:

- Why do we tend to copy what our friends do and say? (*Because we spend a lot of time with them.*)
- What would happen if we spent a lot of time with God? (*We would start to act more like Him.*)
- In what ways might a person become more like God by spending time with Him? (*He or she might be nicer to people, have a better attitude, make wiser choices, or have more wisdom in situations.*)

Conclude by stating that as we spend more time with God, He has an effect on us. As a result, we begin to change into the people He wants us to be.

Option 2: Just Like Jesus. For this option, you will just need your group members. Share the following scenarios about a junior-higher named Joe. (Note: as an option, you can also have two group members pantomime the roles of Joe and Mike as you read it.)

Scenario One: It was morning, and Joe was feeling rushed. He rummaged through his room to find clothes. As he began to get dressed, he didn't notice the Bible he had received at Christmas sitting there on the shelf, just where he had left it on Christmas Day. He finished getting ready for school and ran out the door before his mom even knew he had come downstairs.

At school, Joe was enjoying lunch with his friends when he noticed Mike, a nerdy kid who always sat by himself. Joe began to make comments about Mike, and his friends laughed. The more they laughed, the louder Joe spoke. Eventually, Mike noticed that Joe was making fun of him. He quickly got up and ran off, fighting back the tears.

Scenario Two: It was morning, and Joe was feeling rushed. He rummaged through his room to find clothes for the day. He went to grab his Bible on the shelf, but when he noticed how late it was, he decided he would read it later. So he said a quick prayer, finished getting ready for school, and yelled, "Bye, Mom!" on his way out the door.

At school, Joe was enjoying lunch with his friends when he noticed Mike, a nerdy kid who always sat by himself. Joe's friends began to make jokes about Mike and laugh. This made Joe feel uneasy, but he didn't want his friends to think he was a loser. So, he decided he would laugh along with them, but not say anything about Mike. Mike continued to eat lunch by himself, until he finally walked off to class alone.

Scenario Three: It was morning, and Joe was feeling rushed. But before he did anything, he grabbed his Bible. He talked to God and asked Him to open his eyes to understand what He was about to read, and then turned to Matthew 22:35-40, the portion of Scripture he had selected for the day. Joe read the story of how the Pharisees asked Jesus to tell them what was the greatest commandment. Jesus replied that it was to love God, and that the second was like it: to love your neighbor as yourself. Joe finished his time with God and asked the Lord to help him love others throughout his day. After breakfast, he hugged his mom, said goodbye and went out the door.

At school, Joe was enjoying lunch with his friends when he noticed Mike, a nerdy kid who always sat by himself. Joe's friends all began to make jokes about Mike and laugh. This made Joe feel uneasy, so he stood up, walked over to where Mike was sitting, and sat down next to him. Then he started talking to him. After lunch, both Mike and Joe walked off to their classes.

After you have read each of the three scenarios, discuss the following questions with the group:

- What was different in each of the three scenarios? (*The amount of time Joe spent with God, his actions toward his mom, and his actions to Mike.*)

- What was the difference when Joe spent time with God? (*He showed love to his mom and compassion and friendship to Mike.*)

- Why did Joe's actions and attitude change? (*Joe had spent time with God that morning and read about how Jesus said we should love Him and others. Because he had spent this time with God, he began to act in the way that God wanted him to act.*)

- In what ways might a person become more like God by spending time with Him? (*He or she might be nicer to people, have a better attitude, make wiser choices, and so on.*)

Conclude by stating that as we spend more time with God, He begins to have an effect on us, and we begin to change into the people He wants us to be.

APPLY

Option 1: My Testimony. For this option, you need several gift Bibles, notepaper and a pen or pencil. Ahead of time, choose two group members to come to the meeting ready to share their testimonies (ideally, one male and one female). Ask the volunteers to make sure they include the following three points that are essential to a testimony: (1) What their lives were like before they knew Jesus; (2) how they came to know Jesus as their Savior; and (3) how their lives have changed as a result.

Begin by having the two volunteers come forward and share their testimonies. Afterward, explain that just like these two people, many others in the group have also invited Jesus to be their Savior, and it is the most important decision they have ever made. This decision will help them make it through all the changes they are going through and get through even the toughest changes. Invite anyone who has not made this decision but wants to do so to repeat the following prayer after you:

Dear Jesus, I am a sinner. I thank You for dying for my sins. I ask You to come into my life and to help me to follow and to obey You every day. Amen.

Ask anyone who said that prayer for the first time to come up after the meeting and receive a gift Bible. Write down their names, phone numbers, home addresses and email addresses. Be sure to contact them and to encourage them on a regular basis.

Close in prayer, thanking God that He gave His Son for each of us. Ask Him to help the group members to be faithful in their relationships with Jesus Christ.

Option 2: Cookie Cards. For this option, you need copies of "Cookie Cards" (found on the next page) and some chocolate chip cookies (homemade ones work great!). Ahead of time, copy and cut out the cookies from the handout.

Begin by stating that God will continue to change us as we grow closer to Him. Distribute the chocolate chip cookies, and ask the group members to image that they have just discovered the best recipe in the whole world for chocolate chip cookies. They are so good that they can't stop making them—in fact, the cookies are changing their lives! They are sure their friends have never tasted cookies like these before, so they have begun to share them. Their friends

Cookie Cards

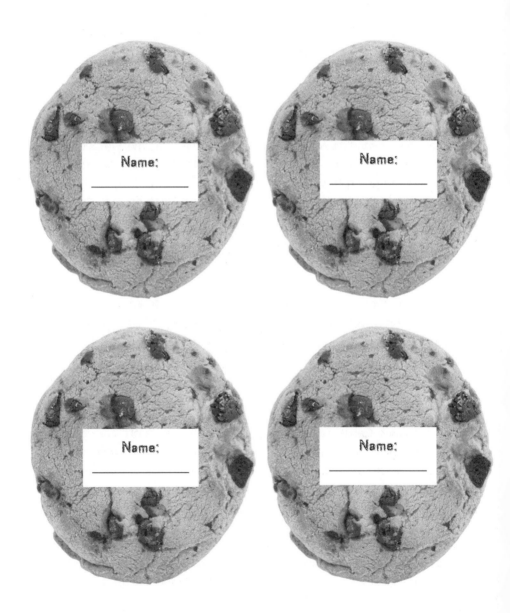

are excited as well, and everyone agrees that the cookies *are* the best in the whole world. There is just one problem. They don't have the time to keep making them for all of their friends. So, what can they do? (*The answer you are looking for is that they can give their friends the recipe!*)

Continue by stating that this chocolate chip cookie is like God. When we share the gospel whenever we can, we help our friends get a small taste of God. Once others have experienced Him, however, they need to know how to keep their relationship with Him going. That is when we share the "recipe"—our own life-changing relationship with God. Ask the group members what are some of the main ingredients in the gospel recipe that they need to share. (*Some answers might include that they will share God loves them, that everyone has sinned, that Jesus is the answer to their sin, and that they have to choose whether or not to commit their lives to Christ.*)

Distribute the paper cookies from the "Cookie Cards" handout and challenge the group members to think of one person in their lives who needs to experience this life-changing recipe. Ask them to write that person's name on their cookie. Encourage them to share the gospel with that person during the upcoming week. Close in prayer, thanking God for the awesome changes He allows us to experience when we grow in our relationship with Him. Also ask Him to give the group members boldness to share the gospel with others.

REFLECT

The following short devotions are for the group members to reflect on and answer during the week. You can make a copy of these pages and distribute to your class or download and print from **www.gospellight.com/uncommon/jh_dealing_with_pressure.zip**.

1—A REALLY BAD DAY

Having a bad day? Psalm 18:2 can help.

You have just had the worst day ever. Your best friend told everyone your biggest secret, your pants split when you bent over in front of the class, you tripped and fell in the cafeteria, your teacher accused you of cheating, and someone shoved you in a locker and left you there for three hours. By the time you get home, you feel like the biggest loser who has ever walked the face of the earth.

What do you do?

- ❐ Completely change your identity.
- ❐ Spend some time telling God how you feel, ask for comfort and read the Bible to remind yourself of God's love.
- ❐ Pretend that nothing bothers you and you don't feel bad.
- ❐ Sit around and watch TV, hoping to forget your problems.

Sometimes you just need a place to run to and hide for a while. At such times, God will be the best place to hide. You can hide in Him by spending time reading the Bible, thinking about how much He cares for you, and asking Him for help. As you look at your own life, what kinds of things make you go to God for help?

_____

_____

_____

Look at Psalm 18:2 again. How is God like a fortress?

_____

_____

_____

In the space below, list some of the things that are troubling you. Then hand them over to God by telling Him about each problem in prayer.

_____

_____

_____

2—GOOD CHANGE

Don't worry . . . read James 1:17 and be happy!

Danny's family had to move to another city, and he was having a tough time dealing with it. He had left behind his friends, his school, his church and the neighborhood where he had lived. Everything was unfamiliar, and he had no idea how to start over in this new place. Sometimes he felt like running away and going back to his old home, but he knew he couldn't make things go back to the way they were.

Sometimes, the changes that occur in our lives are uncomfortable, and we wonder why we have to go through them. However, we have to always remember that God knows what He is doing and that He doesn't make mistakes. Often, He uses these changes to bring us into a new place in our lives so we can grow in our relationship with Him.

What big changes have you gone through recently? Were they easy or hard?

_____

_____

_____

How did you react to the changes? How might you react differently the next time a big change comes?

_____

_____

_____

No matter what happens, God is with you and will never leave you. So today, talk to God about some of the changes that are going on in your life. Tell Him how you feel about them. Ask Him for His help. He will be there for you.

3—SPIT IT OUT!

Turn to 1 John 1:9-10 to read about something truly awesome that God does for us.

Tracy was a little girl who was just learning the difference between right and wrong. One thing she knew was wrong was getting into the cookie jar on top of the counter. However, one day she decided she *really* wanted a cookie. So she got a chair, pushed it up to the counter, and took the cookie. Then she climbed down, pushed the chair back, and ate it. Just then, her mother came into the room. She took one look at Tracy and asked, "What did you do?"

Tracy couldn't hide her guilt. The minute her mom walked in, she knew Tracy had done something wrong. In the same way, we can never hide our guilt from God. While we might get good at hiding it from others as we grow older, God will never be fooled. But the good news is that God understands we will fail, and He has made a plan for it. That plan is forgiveness through Jesus Christ our Savior.

Have you ever tried to hide your guilt from others? Have you tried to hide it from God? What happened as a result?

_____

_____

_____

Do you think your sin affects your relationship with God? If so, in what way?

_____

_____

_____

If you have done something and are trying to hide it, you need to spit it out! Tell God about all your sins—He already knows all about them anyway! Then celebrate, because you can know that you are forgiven.

4—FRIENDS WITH GOD

Read John 15:14-15 to find out what God thinks of you. Then fill in the blanks:

You are my _____ if you do what I command. I no longer call you _____, because a _____ doesn't know his master's business. Instead, I have called you _____, for _____ that I learned from my Father I have _____ _____ to you.

Yes, you read that right—the Bible tells us we can be *friends* with God. Wow! Just think about that for a moment. You can be friends with the all-powerful, perfect, infinite, all-knowing Creator of the universe! But how do you do this?

The first step is to realize that you need God as a friend. Next, tell Jesus that you are sorry for your sins. Third, believe that Jesus has heard you and has forgiven your sins. Finally, decide that you will follow Jesus all the days of your life. When you have prayed and asked Jesus into your life, you have a new Friend and He will never, ever, ever leave you!

Today, thank God that He cares for you and wants to have a friendship with you. Ask Him to help you commit to praying each day and spending some time reading the Bible. Also ask Him to lead you through the changes you are experiencing in your life so you can grow deeper in your relationship with Him!

CHANGES IN OUR FRIENDSHIPS

THE BIG IDEA

As we grow closer to God some of our friendships will change, making it necessary for us to find new friends who will help us to continue to grow and follow God.

SESSION AIMS

In this session, you will guide group members to (1) evaluate their current friendships; (2) recognize that some of their friendships are changing; and (3) see their need to choose friends who will encourage their relationships with God.

THE BIGGEST VERSES

"Let us consider how we may spur one another on toward love and good deeds. Let us not give up meeting together, as some are in the habit of doing, but let us encourage one another—and all the more as you see the Day approaching" (Hebrews 10:24-25).

OTHER IMPORTANT VERSES

Proverbs 17:17; Ecclesiastes 4:9-12; Micah 6:8; John 15:13; Romans 12:10; Ephesians 4:1-3; 1 Thessalonians 2:8; 5:11

Note: Additional options and worksheets in 8¹/₂" x 11" format for this session are available for download at **www.gospellight.com/uncommon/jh_dealing_with_pressure.zip**.

STARTER

Option 1: Best Friend Hangman. For this option, you will need a whiteboard, a whiteboard marker and prizes.

Welcome the group members and divide them into two teams (guys versus girls) for a game of Hangman. Send the teams to opposite sides of the room, and then ask the guys' team to send a team representative forward. When the representative approaches you, ask him to whisper in your ear the name of his best friend from third grade. (Note: that the friend cannot be in the room.)

Draw the number of spaces on your whiteboard needed for the best friend's name. Explain to the group that the guys' team will be guessing the letters that make up the name of the person's best friend. However, the girls' team can win the round at any time by guessing the name before the guys' team does. Each time a letter is guessed correctly, write it in the appropriate space. If a letter that is called out is incorrect, begin drawing the hanged man. Each round is worth one point, so have someone keep score, and award prizes to the winning team.

Alternate rounds between the guys and the girls, changing the questions and bringing up new representatives each time. Play as many rounds as you like. When the game is finished, ask the students to raise their hands if:

- They have the same best friend now that they had in kindergarten.
- They met someone new at their junior high this week.
- They have moved more than once.
- They were able to make new friends right away when they moved.

Explain to the group members that during in their lifetime they will see many friendships come and go. At school, for instance, every time they change classes or start a new school year, they will have the opportunity to meet new people. Today, the group will be learning about friendships and how they affect each of us.

Option 2: Changing Groups. For this option, you will need just this book and your group. Begin by explaining to the group that you will be calling out different topics, to which the students will need to shout their answers. As they do this, they will need to find others who are calling out the same answer and form an answer-based group. For example, if you call out "favorite color," they will shout out their answers such as "blue," "green," "purple," and then find others who are yelling that same color. (Some of the group members may wind up all by themselves—their color might be fuchsia, for instance—but that's okay.)

When everyone is in a group (even if it is just one person), ask the groups to state their favorite color. Next, call out another topic and have the group members repeat the process. Some ideas for topics include: favorite ice cream, favorite sport, favorite music group or performer and favorite animal. Call out several topics to make sure students regroup several times. At the end of the game, have everyone come back to the main group, and then ask for a show of hands if anyone stayed in the exact same group the whole time. (*There shouldn't be any hands raised.*)

Explain that life is a lot like this. People come and go, and often the group we belong to today will not be the one we belong to tomorrow. Many things in life change as we get older—foods we like, hobbies, and even our friends. To illustrate this point, ask the group members to raise their hands if:

- They have the same friends as they had in first grade.
- They met someone new at church or at school this week.
- They have switched schools at least once in their lives.
- They have experienced the loss of a friendship through no fault of their own or the other person—they just drifted apart.

Explain to the group members that during their lifetime they will see many friendships come and go. Sometimes new people will come into their lives with whom they will form close friendships, while at other times some friends will just seem to drift away. This is just a natural part of life, and today we will be looking at how this type of change affects each of us.

MESSAGE

Option 1: Spurs. For this option, you will need several Bibles, a coin and prizes. Begin by dividing the group members into two teams. Have each team sit down in a line facing the other team, with only a small amount of space between them. Have the players on each team hold hands.

Next, instruct the group members to close their eyes, with the exception of the first person in each line, who can keep his or her eyes open. Explain that you will flip a coin, and if the coin lands heads up, the first person in each line will squeeze his or her partner's hand. The partner will pass the squeeze to the next person down the line, until the last person's hand is squeezed. The last person will then open his or her eyes and run to the front of the line. That person now becomes the leader, and the other team members must close their eyes.

The process then repeats with you flipping the coin again *unless the coin landed tails up* and the leader accidently squeezed his or her partner's hand. In that case, the last person must return to the end of the line, and the leader who made the mistake must go again. Note that once the leader has made the mistake, the team must play through and squeeze hands until the last person comes up and tags the leader.

The game ends when the person who was originally last in line becomes the leader (when everyone on the team has cycled through once). Award prizes to the winning team, and then discuss the following questions:

- Why did you squeeze the hand of the person next to you? (*Someone squeezed my hand.*)
- Was your reaction slow or quick? (*Quick.*)
- Why was it quick? (*We wanted to win the game.*)
- What are "spurs?" (*They are spikes riders wear on their boots to make a horse react quickly and go faster.*)
- How does the idea of a spur relate to this game? (*Squeezing a partner's hand "spurred" him or her on.*)

Distribute the Bibles and explain that understanding the concept of "spurs" can help us as we choose our friends. Choose a volunteer to read Hebrews 10:24-25.[1] Explain that the first quality we should look for in a friend is someone who spurs us on or causes us to show love and do good deeds. This person should bring out the best in us.

Ask the group members to think about people in their lives who spur them to do wrong things, such as gossiping, cheating off their tests, and/or even pressuring them to do things that are illegal. Now ask them to think about the friends who not only encourage them but also get them excited about loving Jesus, loving others and doing good. Ask them how they feel about themselves when they are with each of these different types of friends. Who are the better friends in the long run?

Youth Leader Tip

Develop your "foghorn quality." When foghorns go off, captains don't say, "Oh, that foghorn is always spouting off. We don't need to listen." No, they pay attention because they know it knows something that they do not.

Explain that we all need friends who will spur us on to do things that honor God. Who we choose to be our friends is important, because they have an incredible amount of influence in our lives. They influence our choices, our decisions, our feelings and even our relationship with God. When we have friends who encourage us to live in the way God wants us to live, we will find that they actually help us grow in our relationship with God.

Option 2: Lighting the Way. For this option, you will need several Bibles, some strong coffee (enough for each person to have a little bit), small Styrofoam cups, cartons of vanilla- and chocolate-flavored creamers, and a flashlight.

Distribute the Bibles and choose a volunteer to read Hebrews 10:24-25. Explain to the group that as we lose some friends and gain new ones, God wants us to choose friendships that are going to encourage us in our relationship with Him. As this passage reveals, there are two key qualities for a godly friendship. The first is that our friend spurs us "toward love and good deeds" (verse 24).

Hand out the cups of coffee and encourage the group members to take a sip. (Several students will probably protest because of the taste.) After everyone has had a sip, allow them to add some creamer (let them choose the flavor) and invite them to try the coffee again. Their reactions should be a little bit better this time. Make the point that while some of the group members might have liked the taste of the strong coffee, others preferred the taste of the coffee with creamer. This is because the creamer brought out the best in the coffee.

Explain that as our friendships change, we need friends who will bring out the best in us. That includes calling us on stuff that we need to change and encouraging us to do the things God wants us to do. We need people who will get our attention, help us make good decisions, and motivate us to do what is right.

Continue by stating that the second quality for a godly friendship we find in Hebrews 10:24-25 is that our friends should encourage us to follow God. Ask the group members if any of them has ever taken a hike in the dark. Turn off the lights in the room, and explain that if they have, they probably found it difficult to stay on the trail with no light to guide them. Now turn on the flashlight and explain that with a light source, we can not only follow the trail but also show others the way.

Turn the lights back on in the room and choose a volunteer to read 1 Thessalonians 2:8. State that one of the best ways we can encourage someone to walk with God is to walk with Him ourselves. In the same way that we need friends who will encourage us to grow in our relationship with Christ, we need to be a friend who will set an example and show others the way.

DIG

Option 1: The Pull of Friendship. For this option, you will need two strong adult volunteers to be "spotters," and a sturdy chair.

Begin by choosing two volunteers from the group. Have one volunteer stand on the sturdy chair and the other volunteer stand in front of it. Ask them to hold hands. Tell the volunteer standing on the chair that when you say "pull," he or she must try to pull the other person *up* onto the chair. Meanwhile, the volunteer standing on the ground will be trying to pull him or her *down* off the chair. Position the spotters on either side of the chair (to avoid injuries) and say, "pull!" The volunteer on the ground should be able to easily pull the other person off the chair. Have the volunteers switch places and try again. The person on the chair should still be easily pulled down.

Ask the group members if they have ever had a bad experience when they tried to get their friend to do the right thing. If so, they were much like the person standing on the chair. It is very difficult to "pull up" a person who doesn't want to do the right thing, and all to often we will find ourselves instead getting dragged down to their level. This is why we need to have friends who support us and encourage us to do what is right. If we know someone else agrees with us, it's easier to take a stand.

Conclude by asking the group members to take a few moments to think about their current friendships. Are they in friendships that are pulling them down? Or are they in friendships that are lifting them up and strengthening them in their relationship with God? If they are not sure, let them know that they will next be learning how to evaluate their current friendships.

Option 2: A Friend in Need. For this option, you will just need the following case study. Read the following to your group:

> Marco grew up going to church. He went to camps and memorized verses in the Bible. He was also a good athlete who played baseball, basketball and football. Marco was a great quarterback. In fact, he was the first seventh grade starting quarterback in his school's history.
>
> Marco's best friend was Sean. They had known each other forever and used to do everything together, including going to church. But as time went by, Marco found himself spending more time with the guys on the football team and less time with Sean.
>
> The guys on Marco's football team were notorious for being rowdy and causing trouble, and most of them didn't know much about Chris-

tianity. Pretty soon, Marco started skipping church, even though his parents thought he was at youth group. After his Mom dropped him off, he would run across the street to the mini-mart to meet his buddies. Marco felt bad about this, and he didn't like everything his football buddies were pressuring him to do, but he was afraid that if he stopped hanging around them he wouldn't be as popular at school.

One evening, Marco ran over to the mini-mart as usual, but when he got there, he realized he had forgotten his money. "No big deal," one of his buddies said. "Just go in there and take something. We do it all the time." When Marco hesitated, his friends started calling him "chicken" and making clucking sounds.

Marco finally gave in and went into the store, where he began to carefully stuff his pockets with things from the shelves. When he thought no one was looking, he walked out the door. To his horror, a police officer was standing right outside the door. The officer asked Marco to empty his pockets. He was busted.

Now discuss the following questions:

- Before Marco started hanging out with his football buddies, would he have tried to shoplift something? (*Probably not, because his Christian friends like Sean wouldn't have pressured him to do so.*)
- Why did Marco started spending more and more time with the guys from his football team? (*He had fun with them, and he wanted to fit in.*)
- How do you think Sean felt as he watched his best friend slip away into a bad crowd? (*Helpless, sad and even angry.*)
- Who influenced whom more: Marco or his football friends? (*Marco's football friends influenced him more.*)

Read Proverbs 17:17 and John 15:13. Ask the group what they think Marco could have done differently in this situation. (*One answer would be that he could have told Sean about his struggles and asked him for help.*) State that true friends will always motivate us to do what is right, because they have our best interests in mind. Unlike Marco's football buddies, they won't want us to get in trouble, so they won't pressure us to do what is wrong.

Invite the group members to take a few moments to think about their current friendships. Are they in friendships that are pulling them down? Or are they in friendships that encourage them in their relationship with God? Explain that if they are not certain, you will next be discussing how they can evaluate their current friendships.

APPLY

Option 1: Friend Factor. For this option, you will need several Bibles, an adult volunteer, copies of "Friend Factor" (found on the next page) and also pens or pencils.

Begin by distributing the Bibles and choosing a volunteer to read Romans 12:10 and 1 Thessalonians 5:11. Explain that in order for us to be in friendships that encourage us, we need to choose the right friends. This not only means evaluating the people with whom we're friends but also evaluating ourselves.

Divide the group members into teams of five to seven people. Distribute the "Friend Factor" handouts and pens or pencils. Instruct the group members to think of one of their friends and then use the chart in the handout to evaluate the friendship. The list is a tool that can help them evaluate whether or not their friends are encouraging them and whether or not they are being an encouraging friend themselves. Stress that it is important for them to be honest with themselves. It's okay if they don't have all of the characteristics on the list—they can ask God to help them in those areas. Remind them that no one is going to be perfect.

Allow several minutes for the teams to complete the lists, and then encourage them to discuss their discoveries in their small groups and pray about their individual friendship needs. Close in prayer, thanking God for the encouragement and support of good friends and asking Him to help the group members distinguish between friendships that are godly and those that are not.

Option 2: Be Accountable. For this option, you will need copies of "Be Accountable" (found on page 168). Ahead of time, invite two people the group members know and respect to share about their friendship (how they met, how the friendship developed, what obstacles the friendship has overcome, how their friendship has helped them grow closer to God, and so on). Also have the people state how they have been accountable to one another.

Begin by introducing the guests and inviting them to share about their friendship with one another. When they are finished, explain to the group that a good friendship like this demonstrates accountability. Accountability is a system in which two or more people help each other stay focused on their goals in life. As Christians, it's important that we have people in our lives to whom we

Friend Factor

Does your friendship "hit the mark"? Put an X in the box that represents the best answer for each question. Then write the number of circles you shaded in the "total" column below.

	1	2	3	4
	YES! Always	Most of the time	Not usually	NO! Never
Does this person have a strong relationship with God?				
Does this person encourage my relationship with God?				
Is this person a good listener?				
Does this person build me up and encourage me?				
Is the person trustworthy?				
Does the person keep secrets and not gossip?				
Does the person accept me?				
Does the person support me when I'm struggling?				
Does the person pray for me?				
Is the person loyal?				
TOTAL				

If you shaded most of the circles in columns **1** and **2**, this is a friend who tends to support and encourage you. If you shaded most of the circles in columns **2** and **3**, this is a friend who is probably not always there for you 100 percent of the time. If you shaded most of the circles in columns in **3** and **4**, this is likely a friend who is not encouraging you, and might want to consider if this person really has your best interests at heart.

BE ACCOUNTABLE

Did you spend quality time with God this week?

Are there any situations that are tempting you?

How are things going in your family?

Are you being a servant in your home?

Are you doing your homework faithfully?

Is there anything I can pray about for you?

are accountable. We need people to ask us tough questions about our relationship with God and the lifestyle we are living.

Distribute the "Be Accountable" handout and state that some of the group members may have friends whom they feel are encouraging and supportive. These are great friendships to take a step further. To this end, challenge the group members this week to consider asking one of these close friends to be their accountability partner. This means the two of them would meet regularly, and during their time together they would ask each other the questions listed on the handout.

Close in prayer, thanking God for the support of good friends and asking Him to help the group members find those friends who will keep them accountable—even when it is difficult to do so.

REFLECT

The following short devotions are for the group members to reflect on and answer during the week. You can make a copy of these pages and distribute to your class or download and print from **www.gospellight.com/uncommon/jh_dealing_with_pressure.zip**.

1—FOREVER FRIENDS

Extra, extra! Read all about it in Proverbs 17:17!

Imagine that some of the other kids at school are making fun of your best friend for being kind of nerdy. You've been friends since elementary school, but lately things have been changing. You've been making more popular friends, and some of your other friends tell you that you should "ditch the nerd." You really care about your best friend, but you wonder if it's time to move on and join the more popular kids.

What do you do?

- ☐ Ditch the nerd.
- ☐ Try to give your best friend a makeover and some tips on becoming more popular.
- ☐ Join in making fun of your former best friend.
- ☐ Stand up for your friend and decide you don't want to be friends with people who make fun of other people.

How would you feel if you were the friend being ditched?

_____

_____

_____

_____

What does it take to stay friends through the hard times?

_____

_____

_____

_____

How can you be a better friend?

_____

_____

_____

_____

Today, do something nice for your friends . . . just to show you appreciate them!

2—SHINE BRIGHT

Don't stop now! Go to Micah 6:8.

Sarah was surprised when Tina wanted to talk to her after school. Tina was *so* popular—and she had a bad reputation. Sarah was even more surprised when Tina confided in her that her parents were getting a divorce. Tina cried and told Sarah how upset she was. Then she said, "Sarah, I don't know you very well, but I knew I could talk to you. Everyone knows you're a Christian, and everyone thinks you do the right thing. I knew you would listen to me and care about what I said."

You may not think anyone notices when you do the right thing. But in fact, they do. In the same way, they notice when you do the wrong thing. While you may be tempted to think it's not worth the effort to make the right choices, people *do* notice your character, and it's always worthwhile to do right. Even when you don't realize it, God is working through you to show other people what being a Christian is all about.

Was there a time when the other kids at school noticed that you did the right thing or that you were a Christian without you saying anything about it? If so, what happened?

_____

_____

_____

_____

According to Micah 6:8, what does God require of you?

_____

_____

_____

_____

Today, pray and ask God to help others see Jesus in you.

3—WHAT'S UP?

Flip open that Bible to Ecclesiastes 4:9-12.

Imagine your grandmother is very sick. You would really like to talk to someone about it, but you're afraid to ask anyone to listen. You always try act like you have it all together. You find it scary to tell others about your problems, because you worry they might not care about what you are facing. What do you do?

- ❑ Keep your problem to yourself and keep pretending everything is fine.
- ❑ Pray about your problem and ask God to make it go away.
- ❑ Tell everyone at youth group that you have an "unspoken request."
- ❑ Talk to a friend about your problem and ask him or her to pray with you about it.

Why are we sometimes afraid to tell others what is happening in our lives?

_____

_____

_____

_____

_____

How can talking to a friend help us deal with problems?

_____

_____

_____

_____

_____

We all have problems that weigh us down. So this week, find a friend and talk with that person about a struggle you're facing. Ask that person to share with you, and then pray together.

4—MAKE IT RIGHT!

Read the rules about being a friend in Ephesians 4:1-3.

The youth group was devastated when their youth pastor announced he was leaving. Some of the students said they wouldn't come to the church anymore. Others said they were mad at the youth pastor for deserting them. "How could he leave us?" they asked. "Doesn't he care about us? What's going to happen to our group?"

The youth pastor reminded them, "God is the leader of this group, not me. Now, more than ever, you guys need each other. You need to be unified and to support each other to keep the group together."

We really do need each other, and God wants us to be in unity so we can show others His love. He is our leader. Below, make a list of the rules for getting along that are listed in the Ephesians 4:1-3:

1. Live a life_____ of the _____ you have received (verse 1).

2. Be completely _____ and_____ (verse 2).

3. Make every effort to _____through the _____ (verse 3).

We are a family—the family of God. While each of us may have different ideas and different ways of doing things, we must learn to get along and act as members of the same family. So if you are upset with another member of God's family, go to that person today and make it right!

CHANGES IN OUR RELATIONSHIPS WITH PARENTS

THE BIG IDEA

As we grow older we need independence, but we should still honor our parents.

SESSION AIMS

In this session, you will guide group members to (1) understand their desire for more independence; (2) learn what the Bible says about their responsibility to honor their parents; and (3) respect their parents in new ways this week.

THE BIGGEST VERSES

"Children, obey your parents in the Lord, for this is right. 'Honor your father and mother'—which is the first commandment with a promise—'that it may go well with you and that you may enjoy long life on the earth'" (Ephesians 6:1-3).

OTHER IMPORTANT VERSES

Exodus 20:12; Deuteronomy 5:16; Proverbs 12:15; Matthew 7:9-11; John 14:15; Romans 1:28-32; Colossians 3:20

Note: Additional options and worksheets in 8$^1/_2$" x 11" format for this session are available for download at **www.gospellight.com/uncommon/jh_dealing_with_pressure.zip**.

STARTER

Option 1: Water Wars. For this option, you will need an outdoor space for a water fight, three red markers, three blue markers, lots of children's watercolor books (the kind where you just add water to bring out the color), two road cones, masking tape and lots of red and blue water balloons. Ahead of time, put together two sets of supplies (red items for the red team and blue items for the blue team) of all the items you have. Put the two road cones on opposite sides of the playing area, which will stand for the two team's home bases. Put one set of supplies at each base.

Welcome the groups and tell them that they will be playing a game called "Water Wars."[1] Divide the group members into two teams. Designate one team as the red team and the other as the blue team, and have each team go to its home base. Ask each team to begin taping pictures from the watercolor books onto the backs of its team members while you explain the game. Each player will begin the game with this watercolor picture taped to his or her back.

Explain that each team's objective is to prevent the capture of its "treasures" (the three felt-tip pens). The team treasures must remain near the traffic cone in plain sight (no putting them in pockets or hiding them), and a team can only capture one treasure at a time. When a player captures one of the other team's treasures, he or she must take it back to his or her own home base, where it will be held hostage until a player from its own team can rescue it.

Teams will defend their treasures by hitting opponents with water balloons. When a player is hit by a water balloon, his or her watercolor picture should begin to show colors. When this happens, the player must stop immediately until another team member can successfully tape a new picture onto his or her back (while avoiding the bombing, of course!). If a player has possession of an opposing team's treasure when he or she is hit, the opposing team can recapture the treasure, but only *before* a new picture is taped to the player's back.

When everyone has a picture on his or her back, give the signal for the game to begin. Stop when a team has successfully captured all three of its opponents' treasures. Declare the winners, and then ask the group members to raise their hands if they were tempted to break a rule, such as running even when they were hit by a balloon. Next, discuss the following questions with the group:

- Why do you think we have to obey laws that tell us what we can and can't do? (*Laws protect people from getting hurt, and they bring order.*)
- Why do people disobey laws designed to keep them and others safe,

such as speed limits and traffic laws? (*They are in a hurry, they're not paying attention, they don't care, and so on.*)

Explain that most people feel they have a *right* to break some laws, because they don't think their actions will hurt anyone. Perhaps some of the group members' parents have set rules for them that they are starting to question. They wonder whether or not those rules should really apply to them. Now discuss the following:

- What is one rule your parents have at home that you don't think you should have to follow anymore? What is the rule?
- Has anyone here ever broken that rule?
- Have you ever tried to negotiate new terms with your parents for the existing rule?

Conclude by stating that as junior-highers, it is understandable that they want to start making their own decisions and choices. The problem is that it's wrong to disregard their parents in this quest for independence. Today, the group is going to look at the changing relationship that is happening with their parents and try to figure out together how God would want them to respond.

Option 2: Chain of Command. For this option, you will need a large open space and some prizes.

Begin by welcoming the group members, and then choose a volunteer to be "It." (Note: If your group is larger than 15, designate one person to be It for every 15 players.) Explain that in this game they are going to be playing, It will try to tag as many people as possible. If a player is tagged, he or she will link arms with someone else who has been tagged, and they will begin to form a human chain. The chain will also be able tag players, but everyone's arms in the chain must remain linked—no breaking the chain to tag someone. The game is over when only one person remains untagged (besides It, of course).

Once the game is finished, have the group members come back to the main area. Discuss the following questions:

- When you were in the chain, what made it difficult to tag people? (*You had to stay connected, and people wanted to go in different directions.*)
- Was anyone tempted to let go of the chain to tag someone?
- Did anyone actually give in to the temptation?

Explain that as this game shows, it is sometimes hard to stay within the limits of the rules. We all like to go out on our own and at times do what we want to do. Perhaps the group members have noticed this with their parents, especially in the area of rules that their parents set. Many of them might be questioning some of these rules and wondering why they have to follow them now that they are older.

Ask the group members to name one rule at home that they don't think they should have to follow. (Answers might include *bedtime, curfew, or no doing homework in front of the TV*). Now ask if any of them has ever broken one of those rules. If so, what happened? Have they ever tried to negotiate "new terms" to the rules? Did that effort end in success, or did their parents push back?

Explain to the group that as junior-highers, they are beginning to want to make their own decisions and choices about their lives. However, as they do this, they need to make sure that they are honoring their parents. To this end, today the group is going to look at their changing relationships with their parents and try to figure out how they can still obey them as they continue to grow in their independence.

MESSAGE

Option 1: Words with Friction. For this option, you will need several Bibles, prizes and a coin to flip. Begin by dividing the group members into two teams by gender (boys in one team, girls in the other). Choose two guys and two girls from each team to be the players, and then designate one player from each team who will be #1 and one player who will be #2. Flip a coin to see whether the guys or the girls will play first.

Explain that in this game, you will whisper a word to each team's player #1. Each team's player #1 will receive a different word, and the words will be the name of something that is part of their home lives *and* something that can cause friction between them and their parents. For example, some items might include the TV remote, the vacuum cleaner, curfew, parties, movies, brothers, dating and so on.

The player from the team that gets to go first will then say a one-word clue aloud, and his or her teammate will try to guess what the word is. If the teammate guesses correctly, that team wins 1 point. Note that the clues player #1 gives can't use any part of the word (for instance, if the word is "dishwasher," the clue can't be "dishes"). If player #2 guesses incorrectly, the turn goes to the opposing team. Player #1 from the opposing team will then give a one-word clue to help his or her teammate guess their team's word. Explain that any help from the audience will cause points to be deducted from the team that interfered.

Go as many rounds as you have time (or words) to play. When the game is finished, award the winning team prizes. Explain that all the words in this game related to things a junior-higher might argue about with his or her parents—things that might cause friction between them. However, God has something to say about our relationships with our parents.

Distribute the Bibles and choose a volunteer to read Ephesians 6:1-3.[2] Explain that the command to honor our parents should not be taken lightly—it's even one of the Ten Commandments (see Exodus 20:12)! God says we need to obey our moms and dads. Of course, there is a price to pay for doing so—we won't always get our way, and we might have to demonstrate responsibility before our parents give us more freedom. However, honoring our parents will give us many benefits, such as peace in the home, learning from our parents' experience, and earning their trust over time. The question for us is whether the benefits are worth the cost. We will explore this issue today and also look at some of the consequences for *not* obeying our parents.

Option 2: The Great Parent Debate. For this option, you will need to have several Bibles.

Distribute the Bibles and explain to the group that God has something to say about our relationship with our parents. Choose a volunteer to read Ephesians 6:1-3. Explain that in this passage, Paul is giving us a command that shouldn't be taken lightly—in fact, it's even one of the Ten Commandments (see Exodus 20:12). But notice what else Paul says: "Honor your father and mother . . . that it may go well with you and that you may enjoy long life on the earth." From this, we see that not only is honoring our parents what God wants us to do, but we will receive benefits for doing so. To figure out some of these benefits, we're going to have a little debate.

Draw an imaginary line down the middle of the room. Tell the group members to your left that they are going to argue for being able to do whatever they want. Those on the right are going to argue for the benefits of obeying their parents. Allow a few minutes for the group members to come up with arguments, and then begin the debate. Make sure the following benefits are covered: (1) Parents have been there before, and they can learn from their experiences; (2) there will be less arguing and fighting if they obey their parents; and (3) in the long run, they will gain independence the right way.

Conclude by stating that when we choose to honor our parents, there is both a reward and a cost. The cost is that we won't always get our way, and we might have to show responsibility first before our parents give us more freedom. The benefits, as we have seen, are that we gain wisdom, have peace in the home, and get our freedom and independence the way God intends. So, do the rewards outweigh the cost? Before we answer that question, we have to learn a bit more about what the consequences might be if we decide *not* to honor our parents.

DIG

Option 1: Make the Rules. For this option, you will need a whiteboard, a whiteboard marker, paper, pens or pencils and prizes. Ahead of time, draw a line down the middle of the whiteboard and label the left column "rules" and the right column "consequences."

Divide the group members into teams of five or six people and distribute paper and a pen or pencil to each group. Explain that they will now be playing a game in which they must come up with as many rules for their team as they possibly can. The more rules they come up with, the better. Give a signal for the teams to begin, and allow three to five minutes for them to brainstorm the rules and write them down.

When time is up, ask the teams that came up with 1 to 5 rules to raise their hands. Next, ask the teams that came up with 6 to 10 rules to raise their hand. Then ask the teams that came up with 10 to 15 rules to raise their hands. You get the point—keep going until you are left with one group that has the most rules (or a tie). Reward the prizes to the group(s) with the most rules, and then ask the teams to share some of the rules they brainstormed. As they share, write them in the left column on the whiteboard.

When you are finished, ask the group to help you think of all the consequences that could occur if these rules or guidelines were not followed. Write the responses on the right side, and then ask for a show of hands to the following questions:

- How many of you have ever done something that your parents asked you not to do?
- How many of you suffered the consequences?

Explain that when we decide to do things our parents have asked us not to do, we are not honoring them. When we make these kinds of choices that disrespect our parents, they will get angry with us, trust us less, and even give us more rules to follow. However, when we choose to obey our parents, they will begin to trust us more, and eventually they will give us more freedom. It may take a while, but in the long run it will be worth it.

Ask the group members to imagine their parents have asked them to do a chore they really don't like doing, such as mowing the lawn, or folding the laundry, or cleaning the cat litter. To them the task seems really unfair because their younger brother or sister *never* has to do anything around the house. In this situation, what can they do? Well, while there are several courses of action open to take, the best one would be to obey their parents at the time and then discuss their frustrations at a later time when less is at stake. This will show their parents a lot of respect and will go a *long* way toward earning their trust.

Explain that when the group members do bring up the issue later, they need to talk to their parents about their feelings, present their case, and let their parents know in a respectful way why they think the situation was unfair. Again, the more they respect and honor their parents, the more likely their parents will be to hear them out and maybe alter their decisions in the future. This will earn the group members greater responsibility, respect and, eventually, independence. In the long run, life will be much better for everyone if they follow God's command to obey their parents.

Option 2: Dressed to Dishonor. For this option, you will need just this book. Begin by sharing the first part of the following case study:

> Brandy and her brother, Steve, were excited about the school dance. They rushed down the stairs and on their way out the door yelled "bye!" to their mom and stepdad.
>
> "Brandy and Steven, what on *earth* are you wearing?" their mom asked in astonishment. Brandy was in a short skirt with a tight tank top she had borrowed from a friend. She was wearing a few extra pounds of makeup and was wobbling on a pair of high-heeled shoes she had also borrowed from a friend. Steve had on his baggiest pants, and they were sagging so low you could see most of his boxers over the top. He was wearing a shirt he had borrowed for a friend that he knew his mom would never let him own. His hair was so spiked that it could pop a balloon.
>
> "You are *not* leaving this house like that," their mother said. "You will march right back upstairs and change, or you will not go to the

dance at all." With sour faces, Brandy and Steve glanced at each other and sulked all the way back upstairs to change.

When they reached the top of the stairs, Brandy grabbed Steve. "I've got an idea!" she said.

Ask the group what they think Brandy's idea is and what the two are going to do next. Give the following options, and allow the group members to vote which option they think the brother and sister will take:

1. They decide to obey their mom and wear their own dress clothes.

2. They tell their mom, "Fine, then we're not going to the dance," and then they sneak out anyway.

3. They change into more conservative clothes and hide what they want to wear in their backpacks. When they get to the mini-mart around the corner, they change back into their wild clothes.

Lead the following discussion based on the option the group members chose. If they chose answer 2 or 3, ask the following:

• What would their mom do if she found out what they had done?
• What effect would that have on their relationship and their home life?

Ask the following questions regardless of which option the group members chose:

• What answer shows the most honor for their mom?
• What would be your advice to Steve and Brandy if they were in the same situation again?

Explain that Brandy and Steve showed their desire for independence by the way they dressed, which was definitely different from what their mom wanted! In the same way, many times our own independent desires are so great that we decide not to honor our parents. However, when we make those choices and disrespect our parents, we create a situation in which our parents start trusting us less.

Ask the group members imagine they disagree with their parents on a particular issue (which shouldn't be too tough for them to do!). Explain that the best course of action for them to take is to obey their parents *at the time of the conflict*, and then return to the issue at a later time. This will show their parents a lot of respect, and it will go a *long* way toward earning their parents' trust.

Conclude by stating that when the group members do bring up the disagreement again, they need to talk to their parents about their feelings, present their case, and let them know in a respectful way what their view is. Once they have expressed what they need to communicate, they should listen to their parents' point of view and let them make their decision. The more they show responsibility and respect to their parents, the more they will receive responsibility and respect—and, eventually, independence. In the long run, life will be much better off for both them and their parents if they show honor and respect.

APPLY

Option 1: Talk It Up. For this option, you need copies of "Talk It Up" (found on the next page) and two adult volunteers who are willing to put together a brief skit. Ahead of time, assign the role of the parent to one adult volunteer and the role of the junior-higher to the other. Ask them to practice the skit and have it ready before the session.

For the skit, have the parent enthusiastically ask all kinds of questions about the junior-higher's school day ("What did you learn today?" "Did anything interesting happen at school?" "Do you have any big projects you're working on?" "How was basketball practice?" and so on). The kid should scowl and respond with grunts and one-word answers. Basically, he or she should have the opposite energy level of the parent.

Introduce the skit by explaining to the group that the scene takes place in the car on the way home from school. Ask the volunteers to act out the skit, and then discuss the following questions:

- What was happening in this situation? (*The parent was excited about finding out what happened at the kid's school, but he or she was not interested at all in talking.*)

- Does this sound familiar at all? (*A few heads should nod. This is a great time to share a memory of your own related to this subject.*)

- How could the junior-higher change this situation so he or she could show honor to the parent? (*He or she could answer the parent's questions and even offer some more information about his or her day. Better yet, he*

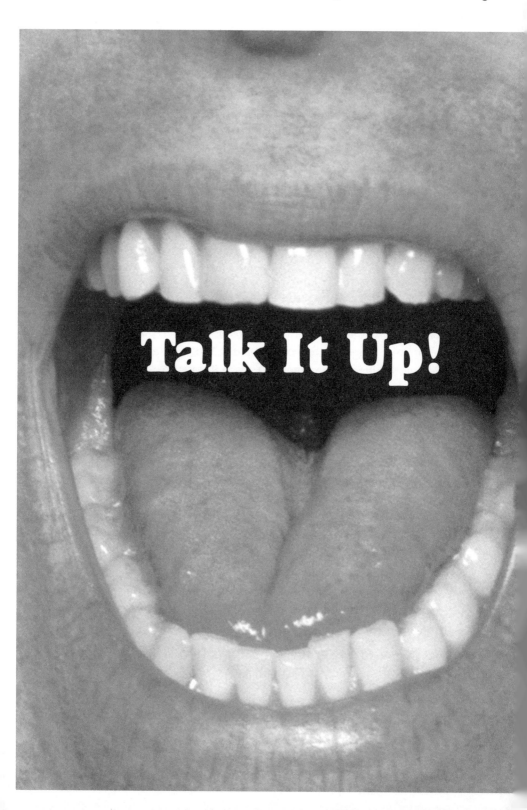

*or she could offer information about the day before the questions begin.
The junior-higher could also ask the parent some questions about how his
or her day went.)*

Distribute "Talk It Up" to the group and explain that communicating with
their parents is a great way to show them honor and respect. Encourage the
group members to make a conscious effort this week to communicate better
with their parents. Instruct them to place their handouts somewhere they can
see them often to remind themselves of the importance of taking the time to
talk with their moms and dads.

Option 2: Just Because Coupons. For this option, you will need copies of "Just
Because Coupons" (found on the next page), pens or pencils, some gift certifi-
cates for free hamburgers or ice cream, a one-foot length of yarn for each student, a hole punch, card stock or construction paper, scissors, glue and
whatever you would like to have on hand to decorate the coupon books. Ahead
of time, copy and cut out the coupons from the handout. Cut out two pieces
of card stock or construction paper to create a front and back cover for the
coupon book. Use the hole-punch to prepare the coupons (six per student) and
covers for the group members to put together a coupon book.

Begin by calling up several students to the front (include some who aren't
typically in the "in-crowd") and give each person a gift certificate. Tell them
that the certificate is a "just because" gift, and then have them return to their
seats. Explain that we all like to receive gifts, especially for no reason at all. When
someone gives us something "just because," it makes us feel special.

Distribute the sets of coupons along with pens, pencils, yarn and supplies
for decorating. State that today the group members have been learning about
dealing with changes in their relationships with their parents. Right now, you
would like for them to think of six things they could do for their parents that
would be "just because" gifts. Some ideas might include cleaning the kitchen,
mowing the lawn, dusting the furniture, babysitting, doing laundry, making
dinner—anything that demonstrates their love, honor and respect for their parents. Have them put each of these six things on separate pages of the coupon
book, decorate them, and then put them together with the yarn.

After the booklets are finished, conclude by stating that their parents will
feel honored by this gift of service. End the session in prayer, thanking God for
parents and asking Him to help the group members honor and respect their
moms and dads.

Just Because Coupons

Just Because

This coupon is good for: _____

It is presented to: _____

From: _____

Just Because

This coupon is good for: _____

It is presented to: _____

From: _____

Just Because

This coupon is good for: _____

It is presented to: _____

From: _____

REFLECT

The following short devotions are for the group members to reflect on and answer during the week. You can make a copy of these pages and distribute to your class or download and print from **www.gospellight.com/uncommon/jh_dealing_with_pressure.zip.**

1—WHAT PLEASES GOD

What pleases the Lord? Find out in Colossians 3:20.

Imagine your best friend is hosting the party of the year. All the important people from school will be there, along with some friends from church. However, when you ask your parents if you can go, they say no because there will be no adult supervision at the party. So you tell your friend you can't go to the party. Just then, your other friend Chris says, "Tell your parents you're spending the night at my house. Then you can go to the party with me!" What do you do?

- ❏ Pack your toothbrush and tell your parents you're headed over to Chris's house.
- ❏ Stay home and invite another friend to come over who also can't go to the party.
- ❏ Ask your parents to supervise the party so you can go.
- ❏ Spend the evening hanging out with your family.

While the Bible isn't clear about what we are to do in every situation, the words of Colossians 3:20 are pretty straightforward: "Children, obey your parents in everything." That doesn't leave a lot of wiggle room, does it? However, the good news is that this "pleases the Lord." If something pleases the Lord, you and He are on the same side, and He will bless you for your obedience.

What are some decisions your parents have made that have upset you?

_____

_____

_____

How did you respond?

_____

_____

_____

How do you think God wants you to respond when something like this happens again in the future? Why?

_____

_____

_____

Remember, God gave you parents for a reason, so the next time they make a decision that bothers you, try to understand why they've made that decision.

2—FREEDOM OF OBEDIENCE

Read Romans 1:28-32 to find out what God says about people who disobey their parents.

When the computer game *Destruction* came out, Nathan knew he had to have it. It looked so cool! But his parents said no, because it was too violent. So, the next time he was at the store with a friend, he bought the game with his own money. Then he hid it in his room and played it whenever his parents weren't around. It was hard to enjoy the game, though, because he felt guilty every time he played it. He always had to watch out for his parents. Eventually, he gave it away to a friend.

The Bible puts disobeying our parents right up there with all kinds of evil stuff. We don't usually think of comparing disobedience with murder, but the Bible does. Why do you think God is so hard on disobedience?

_____

_____

_____

Think of the last time you disobeyed your parents. How did you feel afterward?

_____

_____

_____

How did you resolve the problem?

_____

_____

_____

When you disobey your parents, you may think you're choosing freedom. But in truth, disobedience—like any sin—is really bondage. There is freedom in knowing that you're doing the right thing and you don't have to hide or feel guilty. So, today when you have a choice to obey or to disobey your parents, choose the freedom of obedience!

3—THE PERFECT PARENT

Read about the perfect parent in Matthew 7:9-11.

Your dad promised to be at your track meet to watch you compete. During the event, you look up in the stands to find him, but he's not there. Later, when the meet is almost over, you see him drive up in his car. "I'm sorry," he says. "I wanted to be here, but I had to stay for a late meeting at work. How did you do?" What do you say?

- ❏ "Why don't you ask one of the parents who actually showed up?"
- ❏ "I'm disappointed you didn't show up, but I forgive you."
- ❏ "I did okay. How was work?"
- ❏ Say nothing and refuse to speak to him for a month.

Unfortunately, your parents will sometimes make mistakes. But there is a parent who gives "only good gifts to those who ask him," and that parent is God. He never fails, and He is quick to forgive. And just as He forgives us, we need to forgive our parents when they mess up as well.

In what ways have your parents let you down lately?

_____
_____
_____

How did you respond when your parents did this?

_____
_____
_____

How do you think God can be a perfect parent to you?

_____
_____
_____

Remember that your parents are people too and can't always be perfect. Then, the next time they let you down, let them know how you feel . . . and forgive them.

4—WHAT WOULD YOU DO?

Honor who? Read Exodus 20:12.

Meredith's mom waited in the car while her daughter went up to Katie's house. Katie was going to spend the night. But just as Meredith was about to knock on the door, she heard Katie yelling through an open window, "I don't care what you say! I'm going to spend the night at Meredith's house."

"You will not!" Katie's mom yelled back. "You're sick, you need your rest, and you've been gone every night this week!"

Meredith didn't know what to do. But then she heard Katie yell, "Oh, she's here! See ya!" Katie opened the door and came out.

Meredith took a deep breath. "Katie," she said. "I heard what your mom said. I don't think you should come over today."

Obedience isn't always easy, and it doesn't always seem to make sense. But parents really do want the best for their children, and God commands us to obey them. There is a wonderful promise in the Exodus 20:12. What is it?

_____

_____

_____

_____

_____

Suppose you were the parent and had to make a decision like Meredith's mother had to make—to let her sick daughter go out again or to have her stay home and get the rest she needed. What decision would you make? Why?

_____

_____

_____

_____

Trust that your parents have *your* best interests at heart and go out of your way to obey them today—without complaining!

TOP 10 CHANGES OCCURRING IN A JUNIOR-HIGHER'S MIND

In this unit, we've examined all kinds of changes that will occur in the lives of your group members, including changes in their bodies, changes in their relationships, and changes in their friendships. However, to understand a bit more of how young people process change, it is helpful to understand how their brains are working at this age. The following list reveals the top 10 things you should know about the changes that are taking place in your students' minds and how they affect their decision-making abilities.

1. They Are in a Critical Stage of Development: There are huge leaps in brain development that occur between the ages of 11 to 19. Just as a person will go through a physical growth spurt, he or she will go through a growth spurt in his or her mental abilities as well.

2. Their Brains Are Growing: Junior-highers undergo what scientists refer to as "neuronal sprouting" that peaks around age 11 or 12. Their experiences will shape this new gray matter.

3. They Are Acquiring New Thinking Skills: Because of the increase in brain matter, your students are growing in their ability to process more information than ever before. However . . .

4. They Have Intense Emotions: A young person's decision-making skills will be highly influenced by his or her emotions, because the part of the brain that connects sensory information to emotional responses will not be fully developed yet.

5. They Are More Likely to Seek Conflict: As your group members acquire new skill sets, they will experiment with ways to use them, which often means engaging in conflict with their parents and teachers.

6. They Have Higher Social Anxiety: As young people become better at abstract thinking, their social anxiety increases. They will begin to worry about what others are thinking of them.

7. They Have Trouble Measuring Risk: Young people need higher doses of risk to feel the same rush as adults, and because the part of the brain responsible for impulse control and long-term perspective has not yet developed, they will engage in more risky behaviors.

8. They Need More Sleep: Because of the increase in brain development, their need for more sleep increases—to about 9 to 10 hours each night.

9. They Are More Self-centered and Self-conscious: The hormone changes that occur at puberty, which peak around age 15, make a young person feel as if everybody is watching him or her. While this can make the individual seem self-centered, it can also lead to feelings of self-consciousness.

10. They Are Looking for Structure: While young people will naturally begin to seek independence, they will still desire structure in their lives from parents and other leaders. The best way for adults to provide this structure is to serve as good role models.[1]

Never forget that you can be this positive role model in the lives of your group members. You may not always know what they are thinking—and they may not as well—but know that they will look to you for help and support.